THE
BIRTH
of a movement

De Franco Brocks

Published by:
Movement Material Publishing
Los Angeles, CA
movementmaterialpublishing@yahoo.com

Cover Design: TWA Solutions
First Printing January, 2022
10987654321
ISBN 978-0-578-33833-0

For inquiries contact:
movementmaterialpublishing@yahoo.com

Dedications

This book is dedicated to the memories of my little brother Josiah Elijah Brocks, my little cousin Naima Johnson, my uncle Damian Moore Montemayor, my little brother Joey Jones, my brother Jerald Amaya (a.k.a "Darkside 90042"), my brother Rodrigue Batravil, and all the other family, friends, and acquaintances whose lives were over way too soon. Whether they were taken by way of murder or health issues, I do believe that God takes some of his special souls sooner than later. Either they had served their purpose, or he wanted to save them from the suffering of this world, and to have them look after those left behind.

This book is also dedicated to the ones who helped me become the man I am and supported me the whole way. My mother Dolores Cathrine Montemayor, my father De Franco Van Brocks, my second mom Connie Casey-Holt, my God-mother and Tia Theresa Montemayor, and all of my aunts and uncles who contributed to my life at some point. To all of my cousins who I grew up with and interacted with on a consistent basis. To my sisters Amber Brocks and Amanda Compton-Gordon. To my brother, Silas Brocks and my nephews Isiah, Dominic, Rafael, my nieces Michigan, Tanae, Kahlah, Maya, and Amauri who are an inspiration for the future.

To the love of my life, my wife, Nikki Jones-Brocks who through thick and thin has always been there for me. To my children, Jalen Robert Jerome Ensley, Juwan Antonio Lynn Brocks, Josiah Elijah Felipe Brocks, and Jazmyn Cathrine Rene Brocks. The greatest gift God has given me besides life itself, has been my family. My wife and kids have been instrumental to my life and have contributed more than they will ever know, to the completion of this book.

Finally, to my Movement brothers Marques Jones, Carlos Barriga, Silas Brocks, Ricky Compton, Jerald Amaya, Bruce Roberts, Enrique Guerra, Ryan Rene, Brandon Bradford, Ivan Castillon, Kevin Mayfield, Kelvin Howard, Mike Skilow, and to all the others who have come and gone or have just been around and have contributed and supported in any way. You know who you are.

To my brother, Marques Jones who for almost four decades has been the Yin to my Yang and took up the mantle to take this journey with me. From the birth of the Movement to life, death and everything in between. We have been through a lot (you more than me) and have come a long way. It isn't over yet.

Acknowledgments

I must first acknowledge my Lord and Savior Jesus Christ. Before I knew him personally, he was there protecting me and guiding my way. I am perfect in my imperfections because of his love, his word, and his plan.

I must acknowledge professor Irene Vasquez who contributed greatly to the Foreward with her research paper, "Afro-Latino Influences." What a blessing it was to take a US History class that emphasized the Mexican contribution. Not only did I gain education, I gained inspiration from ELAC (East Los Angeles College) in general and specifically from professor Vasquez. Thank you.

I want to thank CCC (California Conservation Corps) and YCC (Youth Conservation Corps) specifically, for exposing me to God's lands in their most natural form. For taking a chance on a young man like myself, and for teaching me the lessons of teamwork, hard work, how to build things, tear them down, and build them up again. These lessons were both physical and metaphorical.

Mid-City Alternative Magnet School helped to shape who I am and gave me the opportunity to exercise my independent spirit. I have to thank all of the teachers and staff for their dedication, love and support.

Humboldt State University was my first higher education experience and helped me to prove to myself that I was "College Material." I want to thank the professor from my Intro to Journalism class who told me after I got a D in the class that I wasn't cut out for journalism. He was right, I was not meant to report other people's stories, I was born to tell my own.

I have to pay homage to those in Hip Hop that came before us. They paved the way from the east to the west and now, everywhere in between. The elements were forged into the evolution of the culture. The elements sustained individually yet were the fabric of the whole. The art forms are the platforms of expression of the youth and rebellion of systematic oppression.

Finally, I have to acknowledge the haters, the doubters, and the naysayers. Those close to mostly, as well as those detached from the Movement. The ones who couldn't see our purpose, our vision, our aspirations, dreams, and destiny, A.D.D., thank you for the motivation.

$\mathcal{T}$ABLE OF CONTENTS

24 chapters in remembrance of the late great Kobe Bryant, his daughter Gigi, and keeping alive the Mamba Mentality.

FOREWORD

Throughout history, not "his-story," the correlation between Black and Brown people has always been evident yet not as it relates to the writing of the history books. There has always been a driving force and presence that has fought with their every fiber to keep us apart. Let us take the story of the Alamo, for instance. Forget what you know, be it through those same "his-story" books or folktales or movies. The most important thing that I have ever learned about the Alamo was that after the Mexican Army had finally taken it over, there were only three types of people that were spared: white women, their children, and slaves. There was a white woman (Susanna Dickinson), her daughter (Angelina), and a Black slave. The slave's name was Joe and was the "*property*" of the Alamo's commander, William Barret Travis. It is said that there were fourteen or more total survivors, ranging from more women, children, slaves, as well as civilian non-combatants and soldiers, that were used as couriers. This is a story that tells the difference between honor and integrity versus savagery, which has always been a false stereotype of Black and Brown people.

De Franco Brocks

The Spanish Conquistadores
Nicholas De Ovando (1502-1505)
Hispaniola (Haiti/Dominican Republic)

The most unfortunate of the many similarities between Black and Brown people, are slavery and genocide. From African slaves that were shipped over like products from West Africa to those so-called Native Americans (Indigenous) that became slaves or who survived the diseases that caused countless numbers of deaths, 90% of the native population to be exact. "His-storians" have never told the true tale of the Africans and Native Americans (Indigenous) who refused to be enslaved. The ones that were slaughtered with their honor worn and displayed like a badge or a military stripe.

The Spanish Conquistadores
Ponce De Leon (1508) Puerto Rico (Rich, Poor)

The relationship between Blacks and Browns dates to the time that the first African slaves arrived in the western hemisphere. From the Americas to the Caribbean, where African slaves were dropped off for labor purposes, the native occupants who were forcefully integrated by the French and Spanish, eventually integrated with the African slaves. Afro-Latino was born, Puerto Rican was born, Cuban was born and Black-and- Brown was born.

The Birth of a Movement

The Spanish Conquistadores
Juan De Esquival (1509) Jamaica

When I attended East L.A. College, I was privileged and blessed to take a U.S. history class taught by a professor by the name of Irene Vasquez, with a style that emphasized the Latino influence and contributions to this modern United States society. After meeting with Professor Vasquez and informing her about my passion for our "Black and Brown Movement," she gave me a copy of a research paper she wrote entitled "Afro-Latino influences."

The first line read, "Afro-Latinos are integral to the broad ranges of Latin American cultural developments; however, their integration and contributions are not fully recognized." She went on to discuss the demography, economic legacies, political formations, popular culture and introduced the above Afro-Latino (Black and Brown) influences and contributions to historical realms. The term Afro-Latino emphasizes African descent and relates to the Latin American cultural presence to the geography of the peoples.

The Spanish Conquistadores
Alonso De Ojeda (1510) Venezuela

African presence exists in all Latin American societies and only recently have scholars and historians started to take notice and admit African genealogy to be the core component of mixed-race peoples found early throughout Latin America.

It was Iberian Europeans that began forcefully introducing Africans to the western hemisphere. Two-thirds of all Africans brought to the Americas went to Latin America.

The Spanish Conquistadores
Diego Velasquez (1511-1514) Cuba

Back to the beginning, back to the basics, and back to the source; this will take us back to the first and foremost contributions of Africans and Afro-Latinos in particular, which was their labor. Africans and indigenous peoples formed bonds that can be attributed to the oppression suffered under colonialism. Tainos (an area of people) were being accused of sheltering runaway slaves in an area known as Haiti. Therefore, the Iberian European officials of the crown fought to keep African slaves and indigenous peoples apart as their unity threatened the safety of the small Spanish colonial communities. Africans and indigenous people shared a lot of cultural values regarding the importance of family, children, and elders. As stated in "Afro-Latino Influences," they stressed economic cooperation over competition and selfishness. They revered nature and ethical behavior as they would sacrifice for the common good. Although Spanish officials used African slaves to oversee native laborers, they also made colonial laws that granted free status to children of mixed-race populations and products of African slave men and free native women. "Free people of color were people of mixed African, European, and sometimes Native American descent who were not enslaved. They were a distinct group of free people of color in the French Colonies, including Louisiana (New France) and in settlements on Caribbean islands, such as Saint Domingue (Haiti), St. Lucia, Dominica, Guadeloupe, and Martinique." (Wikipedia)

The Spanish Conquistadores
Nunez De Balboa (1513) Panama

The presence of people of African descent were showing in areas from south Florida to Veracruz to Mexico to Buenos Aires and Argentina. These people found refuge from oppressive conditions, fleeing colonial production sites, and established independent communities in many areas of the Americas.

The Spanish Conquistadores
Ponce De Leon (1519) Florida

The cultural transfusion was present in the social organization and religious practices that blended African, Afro-Latino, Afro-Mestizo, Native, and Iberian European/Spanish. "Candomble" is a word that describes an annual religious feast during the colonial period. Afro Bahian religious devotions incorporated recognition of the "Orixas," spiritual energies of forces and ancestor veneration. The devotions helped to transcend political formations, Professor Vasquez stated "worldwide and local crisis fueled the momentum for independence and are the immediate historical context for the social development of Afro-Latino." It was the Haitian people who were first to struggle for and were successful in gaining their independence. This, of course, influenced other Latin American independence movements.

The Spanish Conquistadores
Hernan Cortes (1519-1527) Mexico

This points us to Jose Antonio Paez, who was a "llanero" leader and was of African and native descent. He became the first president of Venezuela. There were numerous military leaders on both sides of the independence/resistance movements that revered Afro-Latinos and soldiers primarily of African descent. It was the "independistas" who pledged to end discrimination and even slavery. Groups of elite Black soldiers were recruited to fight against Spanish forces, including Martin and Artigas.

Simone Bolivar deployed forces with men of African descent and in Mexico; there were numerous Mulattos within the forces of Miguel Hidalgo and Jose Maria Morelos. Independence expressed the possibility of modern political identity in being citizens of new sovereign countries. National identities began to overlap the older racial and ethnic affiliations. The wars that came and went accelerated the travels of Afro-Latinos to isolated areas and kept them concentrated in urban centers.

Modern times brought about a metamorphosis and, even more, an evolution of Afro-Latino. Professor Vasquez wrote, "Diasporas continued in contemporary times. Modern migrations of Afro Carabienos to mainland Latin America during the late nineteenth century and early twentieth century infused central American populations with Caribbean Afro-Latino settlers and Spanish speaking Blacks." There were Black Jamaicans who migrated to Costa Rica, Belize, Honduras, Guatemala, and Panama. They worked on the railroads and agricultural plantations. Jamaicans and another West Indian

Blacks worked on banana plantations. Native/indigenous, Afro-Latino, and people of African descent have and always will have in common, the English, French, and Spanish. Somehow, they were still able to maintain some semblance of their cultures and religions and dialects.

The Spanish Conquistadores
Hernandez De Cordoba (1524) Nicaragua

At the turn of the twentieth century, after years of struggle, Caribbean regions such as Puerto Rico, Cuba, and the Dominican Republic were finally able to overcome colonization. It was not until 1981 that Belize gained its independence. It was the political inspirations of Afro-Latinos that influence the social ideals, values, and principles we can see today. Afro-Latino influences, of course, without question, throughout time have affected modern popular culture. That time frame includes five hundred years of language, music, folklore, and cuisine (foods) and populations as well as many regions of the United States. This again brings us back to the similarities of Black and Brown from Africa to Aztlan (southwest) region of the United States. The one sustaining source of power for these peoples has been music. The inspiration is grounded in the yearning for freedom and justice associated with an ideal society.

In the 1920s, some Afro-Latino communities within the Caribbean began a literary arts movement based on the rediscovery of African heritage, and it was called Negritude. "French Negritude, literary movement of the 1930s, 1940s, and 1950s that began among French-speaking African and Caribbean writers living in Paris as a protest against French Colonial rule and policy of assimilation. Its leading figure was Leopold Sédar Senghor (elected first President of Senegal in 1960) who, along with Aimé Césaire from Martinique and Léon Damas from French Guiana, began to examine Western values critically and to reassess African Culture." (Britannica)

Those who were nearly stripped of everything under slavery were too heavily entrenched in their musical heritage to lose that as well. There are too many instruments, such as the "marimba" and the "Cajon" that are attributed to Africa and are widely acknowledged. There are too many genres, such as "mariachi" music (a well-known tradition of central and western Mexico) that has an African-influenced context. There have been and are too many artists that have and will incorporate African and Native rhythms within their international musical forms.

"Rumba" is an Afro-Cuban-based dance form that has its roots in the Cuban provinces of Havana and Matanzas. It has been said that African slaves that were taken to Cuba in the sixteenth century introduced "rumba." "Timba" is a contemporary Cuban-generated musical form that uses an electric influence and is based on "salsa" and incorporates "Rap" and "R&B."

When speaking about dances such as the "tango" of Argentina, the "samba" and "lundun" of Brazil and the "cumbia" of Mexico and Central America, we speak about African-based rhythms and dancing forms. There were as well, too many Afro-Latino authors, such as Manuel Zapata Olivella and poet Jorge Artel, who have written specifically about the Afro-Latino experience and history. Olivella, who wrote such titles as "A Saint is Born in Chima'," "Chango", the "Biggest Badass," and "Chambacu': Black Slum," is considered one of the greatest Afro-Latino writers of the twentieth century. He sought to communicate with writer Langston Hughes, who was a pioneer of Black literary works. Hughes eventually established friendships with several Afro-Latino authors, including Mexican poets Xavier Villaurrutia and Carlos Pellicer. It was Pellicer who wrote a poem, "Surgente Fin," about the close bond between Africa and Mexico.

De Franco Brocks

The Spanish Conquistadores
Christobal De Olip (1524-1525) Honduras

There were many visual artists, such as Reuben Galloza of Uruguay and Pancho Fierro of Peru, whose still image art depicts the everyday scenes in Afro-Latino urban communities. There are many moving images presented by and for Afro-Latino filmmakers and documentarians who have shown African-based cultural traditions and contemporary experiences. There were many films such as "When the Spirits Dance Mambo" that showed Afro-Latino culture and its interaction with mainstream class and race politics that reminded audiences of the legacies of racialized African slavery.

As stated by Professor Vasquez, "Puerto Rican salsa musician Raphael Cortijo Verdejo pioneered the sound of the "bomba" whose popularity is based on its mastery of diverse musical forms of the Americas, including African based drumming patterns." The legacy he left was as much about his social efforts as it was about his musical innovations. He fought for the improvement of wages and accommodations for Black and Mulato musicians of his era, area, and genre. The fusion that is Afro-Latino started out racially and moved culturally through music, dance, visual arts, and writing. Sports have always been a huge part of American culture and there is no denying the transitional injection of Afro-Latino players into the great "American" pastime called baseball. After all, Latino identity and consciousness is a combination of the heritage and the contemporary story/true history of its people.

World movements for solidarity served to mobilize Afro-Latino activists whose ideals were grounded in past injustices and discrimination

The Spanish Conquistadores
Pedro De Alvarado (1524-1527) Guatemala

Cultural organizations and institutes popped up in the Caribbean, Mexico, Uruguay, Peru, and Argentina with the purpose of educating and disseminating the materials on the African presence in Latin America. There is an annual Afro Caribbean festival that brings scholars, artists, and community members together from Mexico to the Caribbean and South America to highlight the heritage of Afro-Latino in a global context.

The Spanish Conquistadores
Francisco De Montejo (1527-1532) Yucatan

"The efforts by Afro-Latino peoples in the hemisphere to highlight social and economic justices have impacted the agenda of U.S. Congressional officials," wrote Professor Vasquez. Black activists in Columbia formed a Columbian Congressional Black Caucus in 2003 to push for social justice for Afro-Latinos. In 1988, Brazil recognized the rights and status of descendants of runaway African slaves in its constitution. The efforts that came out of Latin America carried over to African American political officials such as congressional representatives.

The Spanish Conquistadores
Antonia De Berrio (1592) Trinidad

The research and findings eventually lead to congressional resolution 47, which reads: "Acknowledging African descendants of the transatlantic slave trade in all the Americas with an emphasis on those descendants in Latin America and the Caribbean recognizing the injustices suffered by the African descendants and recommending that the United States and the international community work to improve the situation of Afro-descendant communities in Latin America and the Caribbean. The last sentence written by Professor Vasquez in her paper "Afro-Latino influences," read "For Afro-Latinos, the recognition of their history and cultural influences in the Americas is an essential part of their struggle for dignity and justice."

It has and always will be of the utmost importance that we as a movement emphasize and focus our efforts on educating the masses on the effects and influences of our Black and Brown peoples in our International and multi-cultural global community.

The background information and history lesson provided are a prelude to the story that is to follow and is an attempt, as has always been the case, for me to take it to the source. When I was old enough to formulate my own thoughts and have the questions that led me to inquire about my roots and where I came from, it led me back to Africa and then here to Aztlan. (Southwest)

I want to thank Professor Irene Vasquez for her insight and contribution to this foreword via her research paper, "Afro-Latino Influences." It is my sincerest aspiration that this is the background and transparency that is needed to divulge on the journey that is to begin with this story, our true story and not "his-story."

This story is about more than just a group of kids who met and grew up and into a brotherhood and eventually a movement. It is about how they met and how they recognized their surroundings and did not fear what they saw, but how they embraced it.

They did not realize how much of an impact music and Hip-Hop specifically would have in their lives. They knew they would be met by some resistance but did not know how much and did not realize it would be just as much spiritual as it would be worldly.

Hip-Hop's history and chronological timeline in comparison to that of the Movement's.

1970 – The "Last Poets" released their debut album, which was a combination of funk music with society-conscious spoken word.

1970 – The birth of Marques Dranae Jones A.K.A Madverblz (One of the Founding Fathers of the Movement)

1970 – Clive Campbell A.K.A "DJ Cool Herc" began deejaying parties in NY and came up with the infamous "Break Beat"

1972 – DJ "Hollywood" began rhyming over popular disco beats

1972 – The birth of De Franco Felipe Brocks A.K.A THC (One of the Founding Fathers of the Movement)

1974 – A former gang member turned DJ named Afrika Bambaataa met a young graffiti artist by the name of Fab 5 Freddy who was a regular on the up-and-coming hip-hop scene. Soon after, Bambaataa formed the Zulu Nation and categorized what he called the 'Four Elements' of hip-hop: DJing, Breaking, Graf Art, and MCing

1974 - DJ Kool Herc coined the term "break-boy" to describe dancers that would dance during his extended breaks in the music. Soon, the term is shortened to b-boy, and the style was called 'breakdancing.' Herc also took an up-and-coming DJ named Grandmaster Flash under his wings. Grandmaster Flash began working on a new, revolutionary technique of DJing. In addition to extending the break of a song, he began mixing parts of two different songs together. Using headphones, he was able to get the songs to overlap and connect. His new 'mixing' technique would be adopted by every hip-hop DJ to follow.

Flash's partner, Mean Gene, had a thirteen-year-old brother named Theodore that also began to DJ at local parties. After he accidentally slid the record under the needle, a young Grand Wizard Theodore took DJing a step farther by pushing the record back and forth lightly under the needle during breaks. He called his new technique "scratching."

1975 - A group of party promoters called the Force stumbled across a young DJ named Kool DJ Kurt. One particularly bold and aggressive member of the Force was a young man named Russell Simmons.

1976 - The Legendary Rock Steady Crew of break-dancers is founded in the Bronx. The Crash Crew was one of the first recorded MC crews and was formed in Harlem.

1977 – The birth of Silas "Papa Silo" Brocks (One of the original Young Prophets of the Movement)

Russell "Rush" Simmons moved the Force to Queens and convinced Kool DJ Kurt to start rapping. Simmons decided to change Kurt's name to Kurtis Blow and enlisted his kid brother, Joey, to be Kurt's DJ. Joey changed his name to 'DJ Run.'

DJing, up to this point, was the primary force in hip-hop. It began to take a backseat to MCing.

The Cold Crush Brothers formed after Almighty KG met DJ Charlie Chase. *1979 – The birth of Josiah Elijah Brocks A.K.A JEB ONE (One of the Young Prophets of the Movement R.I.P. 1979-1997)*

Under manager Russell Simmons, Kurtis Blow became the first rapper to sign a record deal with a major label.

Sylvia Robinson founded Sugar Hill Records and, after hearing a bootleg of The Cold

Crush Brothers, decided to put together a rap group called 'The Sugarhill Gang.'

The Sugarhill Gang released 'Rapper's Delight.' Built on a sample of Chic's disco hit 'Good Times' and written by Grandmaster Caz of the Cold Crush Brothers, it went on to become hip-hop's first mainstream hit and America's first exposure to rap music.

*C*HAPTER 1

It all stated for me in 1982.

The film "Wild Style" was released. Showcasing DJs, graffiti artists, breakdancing, and MC battles, (the main elements of hip-hop) it is Hollywood's first foray into hip-hop culture, and it began a small "rapsploitation" period in film history. After Run and D graduated from high school, they enlisted Jazzy Jase, their DJ friend from Hollis Queens, who called himself 'Jam Master Jay'. Russell Simmons decided to change the group's name to Run-DMC, and they began to work on a single. Simmons also lands the group a deal with Profile Records.

B efore I start the story, I want to give you an introduction to the main characters that are intertwined and woven into the fabric of my existence, an extension of who I am. As sure as my extremities are a part of my body, they are attached to my heart and soul. A family tree if you will:

My great-grandfather Captain Gillis, my great-grandmother "Abuelita." (RIP)

My grandmother "Granny Mom" Elizabeth Gillis-Montemayor.

My grandfather Jesus "Chuey" Montemayor (RIP)

My mother Dolores Catherine Montemayor

The father that raised me and who I am named after, De Franco Van Brocks "Pops"

My stepfather Rick Compton, who I never considered a father figure until his last days (RIP)

My biological father (never met or knew him)

My half-brother on my biological Father's side, Jason Roman

My half-brother on my biological Father's side, Dane Williamson.

My brother Silas Brocks (Young Prophet of the Black and Brown Movement)

My brother Josiah Brocks (RIP) (Young Prophet of the Black and Brown Movement)

My sisters Amber and Amanda

My brother by marriage, who I consider my blood brother, Ricky Compton (Young Prophet of the Black and Brown Movement) (Son of Rick Compton)

My big bro/bro-in-law, Marques Jones (Co-Founder of the Black and Brown Movement and Creator of "Positive Minded Apparel" and "Hip Hop 4 the Pih Poh")

My second mother / mother-in-law, Connie Casey-Holt

My wife and the love of my life, Nawakii Jones-Brocks (sister of Marques and daughter of Connie) (Keeping up with the Jones')

All my uncles and aunties and cousins on my mother's side and on the Jones' side (who I grew up with) (most will not, yet some will be mentioned)

I do not believe in the concept of "friends." To me, you are either family or an acquaintance.

So, some of my extended family will be mentioned and when I do mention these people in the story, you will at least know who I am referring to.

I remember when I took a ride with my mother to see where we were going to move to from Glassel Park, near Glendale California. It was my two brothers and I and as we rode by on the RTD (Rapid Transit District) (in the hood known as the Rough, Tough and Dirty/Dangerous) public transportation bus, my mother pointed and said, "That's where we are going to live." It was a dirt lot where the government (HUD/Housing Urban Development) eventually built a complex for subsidized housing. We were the first residents. It had three bedrooms and one and one-half bathrooms, an upstairs (two stories) and had a patio. There was a playground behind our apartment and in the middle of the complex that was gated and had a laundry facility on-site. There was underground parking, and it was like a mansion to us. I think this was the first time my mother gave us a heads up before something happened. You see, growing up, there was not a lot of communication in our household. Moms would make moves and tell us about them as they were happening or after the moves were made. We did not sit down like the families I had seen on TV and discuss things. Communication along with affection, for the most part, just did not happen in our family. We knew she loved us and did everything she could to took care of us. I later in life found out that this was perpetuated from the past and how she was raised, one of many generational curses. We moved in 1982. I was ten years old at the time.

Our address was 4230 W. Adams Boulevard, Apartment 102, Los Angeles, California, 90018, and it was off Adams Boulevard and Crenshaw Boulevard. Adams Boulevard from Edgehill Drive is a hill that levels off just before Crenshaw Boulevard. Our apartment complex was toward the bottom of the hill and next to the "Montclair" car wash. The car wash was infamous for several reasons. One of the main reasons was that the location was used as a hangout/hub for the neighborhood dope dealers, gang bangers, and motorcycle, car, and van clubs. It was always active, especially on the weekends. There was always music blasting out of the low riders or fixed up rides with the shiny chrome rims. The atmosphere was usually lively and upbeat and there was usually a buzz about this car wash that was entrancing as we hung out in it or just walked through it. It is also where my little brothers, Silas, and Josiah, used to hustle their change for candy, snacks, and video games. As my little brother Silas put it, "Things started to change. I wanted to have more money and do more things. That is when somebody said "hey, why don't' you come over here and help me dry off my car? I'll give you a few bucks." Well, at that time I was like cool, and I started getting a few bucks from everybody and started asking if I could wash their cars. It got to a point where in a day I had made like $20 – $30 bucks, just hanging around the car wash. Then I would go across the street to Johnny's Pastrami and get me a Pastrami and some chili fries, because I was a chubby kid and my whole goal was to get something to eat. (Silas laughs) So, I started hanging out at the car wash and talking to the OG's (Original Gangsters) and listening to the OG's and understanding what was going on in the neighborhood and in the community."

If it was not the car wash, Johnny's Pastrami across the street was another hang out. They had one of the best pastrami sandwiches you could ever have! It would melt in your mouth with that dip and some melting cheese, with only mustard and pickles. I know at least back in the days it was the best I had ever had. I heard they are not as good now as they were anymore, not as big, and do not use the same bread rolls. Of course, they had your classic burgers and fries which were also "bomb" (very good). But those chili cheese fries were out of this world! Unfortunately, for as good as their food was back in the day, so was Johnny's as a hang out spot. I say unfortunately since it was a wide-open space and exposed to Adams Boulevard, which made for a perfect drive-by (when gang members would shoot at their enemies while driving by) location. The fact that so many heads (people) from the neighborhood ate and chilled there, again, it was an easy target. It was a death trap with no escape. There were too many that met their demise at Johnny's, and not all were attributed to a drive by. There were those rare bold individuals who probably parked half a block away, in either direction, and walked up to Johnny's to execute their death missions up close and personal.

I remember Sundays when they would stop traffic at the top of the hill at Edgehill Dr. to drag race cars and motorcycles down the hill of Adams Boulevard. There was never a question of how dangerous it was. Just the sheer momentum at about halfway down the hill would create a desperate need for that last one-fourth mile just before Crenshaw to slow down. There were a few accidents over the years of the drag racing, thank God nothing serious.

There were countless more accidents from regular traffic on that hill than there were from the drag racing. I remember my brothers and I would go outside Sunday evenings, just before sunset, and stand on the sidewalk watching and listening to the racers as they lightning bolted by us. We could feel the sonic boom! We could then see the racers meet up at either the car wash or Johnny's, to exchange winnings and the losses.

$\mathscr{C}$HAPTER 2

(1983) *Grandmaster Flash and the Furious Five released 'The Message.' Moving away from hip-hop's party songs and focused on the realities of inner-city poverty. It was a landmark moment for hip-hop. Run-D.M.C. released their first single, "Sucker MCs/It's Like That." With their different sounding beats and hard, aggressive rhymes, signaling the beginning of the end for "Old School" hip-hop. Run DMC was the first rap group to get consistent airplay on MTV and Top 40 radio. A New York post-punk band called the Beastie Boys decided to switch their sound from punk to rap after attending a party thrown by Fab 5 Freddy.*

My sister Amber was born in 1983. I was now eleven and in my prime kid years, some call the "Wonder Years." While I should have been playing outside with my friends, sports or with toys, I was playing in an alley where there were dead bodies. Don't get me wrong, I did play outside with my friends, sports or with toys. We would wrestle in the grass or reenact our favorite Kung Fu theatre movies. In contrast, there was the time we visited my Tia (aunt) and my Primos (cousins) when they lived in the East LA Hazard Projects.

My cousin Marcus (who has the same birthday as me but is a year older) is who I first smoked marijuana with, I think I was twelve at the time. I remember my cousin Marcus presented me with a classic invention, the toilet paper roll pipe. There may be some of you who might know what I am talking about and for those of you who do not, let me explain. How to make a toilet paper roll pipe: (1) get an empty toilet paper roll (2) use a safety pin to punch holes at one of the ends of the roll to create a larger hole (3) get a very small piece of foil, you will place that over the small hole at the one end of the roll (4) punch a few tiny holes in the foil (5) place the marijuana in the foil and while covering the large hole of the roll at the end where the marijuana is, place your mouth on the other hole on the other end (6) light the marijuana, inhale through the one end and slowly remove your hand from the other end.

This was the first time I smoked weed, and all we did was laugh all night. My older cousin Rubin, who should have been a standup comic, was naturally hilarious. His jokes and commentary were amplified by our newfound heightened senses. Every now and then I can still feel the cramp in my side from how hard we laughed that night.

This was the time in my life when things began to turn for me, between my family life and me as a developing individual. My eyes were wide open, mind was curious, and my personality began to take form. I remember beginning to question things I had not before. I was not yet a teen yet had already begun to take an early exit out of childhood. Growing up as the oldest of five and in the environment, I did, caused me to have to grow up faster than an alternative lifestyle.

I was exposed to things I should not have been at a tender age. Watching my elder family members living in survival mode, carrying with them the baggage and damage handed down to them by the ones before them. This caused them to take on and develop unhealthy coping mechanisms: the sexual promiscuity and perversion, the drug, alcohol, psychological, emotional, and physical abuse. This became the norm and even though it felt wrong, it did not shock my system, it was more of an adaption to it as it was part of my surroundings.

$\mathscr{C}$HAPTER 3

(1984) *The film "Breakin" is released; with "Beat Street" coming soon after. Hip-hop was continuing its push into Hollywood." Beat Street" also showcased a young new artist named Doug E. Fresh, who has the uncanny ability to 'beatbox' - mimic musical effects using only his mouth.*

Russell Simmons met a young college kid named Rick Rubin, who was an avid fan of rap music. Together, Simmons and Rubin founded a small record label ran out of Rubin's college dorm room at NYU. They named their new label Def Jam.

U.T.F.O., who were formerly the backup dancers for Whodini, released "Roxanne, Roxanne." It went on to become one of the most popular rap songs of all time and created more than two dozen 'response' songs, including "Roxanne, You're Through," "The Real Roxanne," "Roxanne's Mother," and most notably, "Roxanne's Revenge" by thirteen-year-old Roxanne Shante.

It is said that after he heard an underground single called "Public Enemy #1" by a college radio DJ named Chuck D... Rick Rubin tried to recruit the rapper for his new label.

The Olympics came to Los Angeles in 1984. I was twelve and vividly remember the frenzy the Olympics created in this city. I know the adults were annoyed somewhat by the inconveniences of traffic and other irritants it may have caused, but in the same breath they were excited to watch the events on TV and see and know their city was on display to the world. I remember the buzz in the city at the time, even though I was a kid. I remember being able to visit the Los Angeles Coliseum for the opening ceremonies and how big it was and how many people were there. It was bigger than anything I had seen or experienced in my life to that point.

Then there was the first time I went down the hill of 28th Street, I rolled down it with my friend Tony, who lived in an apartment behind mine in the same complex. He convinced me to follow him down the hill of this street since we were bored with rolling down our hill on Adams Boulevard. I must have been getting close to thirteen at the time. We were on our bikes. Mine was a blue and gold Huffy I had gotten for Christmas. Coasting down the hill, rapidly picking up speed toward the bottom of the hill, I started to lose control and ended up taking out a side-view mirror on a Mercedes Benz. Obviously, I was not as good on a bike at the time yet either. My handlebars bent backwards from the impact, and I bent over them. The biggest problem for me came after I was able to maintain my balance on the bike and instead of going back to see what damage I had done; I continued to my house, where dinner was being served. As I sat at the dinner table, the doorbell rang. There they were a group of kids from the block (28th Street) who I ended up becoming friends with years later. These kids later became members of the Movement and promotional partners of Josiah and Silas. There were Mikey and Sadaka, Allen and Mikey's sister Felicia. At that point though, I hated them, because they told what I had done and of course I got in trouble since my parents had to pay the bill. I can still feel the sting from that ass whipping. I remember thinking about God and knowing I had done something wrong and committed a sin. I was born into Catholicism, was baptized Catholic, had my communion and just before completing my confirmation, I began having questions that were never really answered. I remember that night kneeling just before going to bed and praying five Our Fathers and five Hail Marys and asking God to forgive me for what I had done. Oh yeah, and by the way, my "Showtime" Lakers won the NBA title in 85. I grew up a HUGE Laker fan, which you will be able to tell.

$\mathscr{C}$HAPTER 4

(1985) A young former delinquent named Kris Parker met a social worker who sometimes was a DJ, Scott Sterling (aka Scott La Rock) at a Bronx homeless shelter. The two decided to form a rap group called Boogie Down Productions. Doug E. Fresh recorded his classic single, "The Show," with the Get Fresh Crew and his new partner, MC Ricky D (aka Slick Rick.)

Run DMC released their second album, 'King of Rock.' Like their debut, it was a hit and furthered the collaboration between rap and hard rock. "Walk This Way" Aerosmith

A sixteen-year-old LL Cool J released his debut album, "Radio." It was the first album released by the up-and-coming rap label, Def Jam.

Def Jam financed and released its own rap movie, "Krush Groove". Based on Russell Simmons' life and starring Blair Underwood as Russell, it also starred Run DMC, Kurtis Blow, the Fat Boys and the newly signed Beastie Boys. The film became a hit.

The only father I have ever known raised me until I was thirteen. And while he had battled drug addiction most of his life, mostly heroin, he decided to start smoking "crack" in 1985. A lot of our peoples fell victim to that era. Our small and modest neighborhood resembled an old western town and gangsters resembled outlaw Cowboys. Wild Wild West is what we called it, like the Hatfield's and McCoy's, the Bloods and Crips were in a classic feud. This later morphed into modern warfare and our hood was then dubbed "Lil Iraq." Not regarding the explosions and war-torn buildings, more related to the body count found in the Middle East Region. This was the mid-1980s, where "crack" cocaine and gang activity were at a peak, an all-time high. "The Ghetto Birds" (police helicopters) were sent to hover over our roofs daily and nightly. I remember not being able to sleep some nights as the propellers spun with the speed of a giant hummingbird's wings. The sounds of propellers, gun shots and sirens became common place: it was like wind, firecrackers, and ice cream trucks. Yellow (Police - Do Not Cross) tape never got a second glance. The scent of gun powder started to blend with my memory, like hints of a weekend barbecue. I continued to stay focused on school, hoping that eventually college would be my escape.

I graduated from Mid-City Alternative Junior High School in 1986. I wore my Don Johnson (Miami Vice) outfit and in my speech, I thanked him, claiming HE was my father. My brother Josiah (RIP) also graduated elementary that same day. I have a picture that included my Tia Teresa and a few of my cousins, as well as my Tia Sylvia and a few more cousins, most notably my little cousin Naima (RIP). She was a couple of years younger than my brother Josiah and was also shot and murdered a few years after him by a jealous boyfriend. This was another gut-wrenching tragedy within our family. Living through those times seemed normal for our lives, yet looking back now, I realize it was not at all. I recall a conversation I had with Bruce Roberts (whom will be introduced later) bringing to my attention a book, chapter, and verses in the B.I.B.LE. (Basic Instructions Before Leaving Earth). We discussed it in depth. It had me thinking that there could have been a connection between my ancestors not obeying God and the generational curses I have experienced and seen in my family and the families I have been closest to, experience.

Deuteronomy chapter 28, verse 15: *"But it shall come to pass, if thou wilt not hearken unto the voice of the LORD thy God, to observe to do all his commandments and his statutes which I command thee this day; that all these curses shall come upon thee, and overtake thee:"*

*C*HAPTER 5

(1986) *Queens native MC Shan and his producer cousin, Marley Marl, released the single 'The Bridge.' Although it went mostly unnoticed by the mainstream press, the song became an instant classic in hip-hop circles. It featured stellar 'new-school' production by Marl and clever lyrics in which MC Shan arrogantly anointed his home, the Queensbridge Projects, as hip-hop's new home base. The song raised the attention of the newly formed South Bronx based Boogie Down Productions. BDP's KRS-ONE dissed MC Shan, Marl and Queens equally in his hard-hitting single, "The Bridge Is Over." Thus, igniting hip-hop's first major rivalry on record, leaving fans eagerly awaiting Boogie Down Production's debut album.*

Run DMC released their third album, "Raising Hell." It featured the Aerosmith collaboration, "Walk This Way," and became an instant hit. It was a cultural milestone for hip-hop. The album drove in four more hit singles, "It's Tricky," "My Adidas," "You be Illin'," "Peter Piper," and became the first multi-platinum rap album.

Hip-hop's first White rap group, the Beastie Boys, released their debut album, "Licensed to Ill," on Def Jam Records. It went on to become the best-selling rap album of the decade.

LL Cool J's debut, "Radio," became certified platinum as Def Jam Records became the premiere label in hip-hop.

A new hip-hop duo named Eric B. & Rakim released their first single, "Eric B. Is President," another benchmark moment in hip-hop. Rakim's clever wordplay and complex rhyme schemes ushered in a new era of MCing as an artform.

Run DMC became the first rap group nominated for a Grammy, for best "R&B Vocal Performance."

Salt-N-Pepa, a new female rap group, released their debut album entitled "Hot, Cool & Vicious." It was a moderate hit.

Rick Rubin signed Chuck D. and his newly formed group, Public Enemy, to Def Jam.

When I think about generational curses, Pops, unfortunately, always comes to mind. Like when he decided to change our downstairs restroom into his personal crack smoking den. I knew he smoked weed cause when I was 10 or 11, he had me take a drag off a cigarette and a joint and asked me which one I liked better. Of course, I said the joint. He would bring a couple of friends over to smoke weed and/or drink and hang out. It became a problem when he began taking his friends into the downstairs restroom. Then he began to bring home the neighborhood crack heads, spending more than an hour at a time in there, like an infested hive. This was when my mother decided we needed to leave our home, the hood, and stay with my Tia Teresa (who is also my godmother) and my Primos in the East LA Hazard Projects.

Deuteronomy chapter 28, verse 16:

"Cursed shalt though be in the city, and cursed shalt thou be in the field."

This was a rougher neighborhood than the one I grew up in, which was bad as it could be on its own. These projects were like a gated community (not the private, desirable ones of the suburbs) with one way in and only that same way out, in the worst part of East L.A. Some of the images still haunt me to this day. I remember being outside one evening with one of my cousins and we saw three men run past us. The first man was younger, maybe early twenties. The next was older and the last man was also younger. The first man had nothing in his hands, the second older man was running with a shotgun in his hands, and the third man behind the second had a bat in his hand. Of course, we did not follow them, but we later found out, the first man was the youngest son of the second man, who was the father of both the first and third man. For whatever reason, the father was chasing his youngest son with a shotgun, while his eldest son chased him with the baseball bat. We heard later that night that the eldest son beat his father with the bat to get the shotgun away from him. Those types of images unfortunately became common place in my childhood. The nightmarish and inconceivably negative realities embroidered in my memory banks forced me towards and helped me to develop a love for reading and writing, which I used as an escape.

(A random journal entry)

"This is not a letter; this is not a poem. This is not a rhyme. This is De Franco Felipe Brocks-Montemayor-Williamson. This is

*when I am in my best form and fashion. This is when I have total
control. When I write, I leave this world that leaves me scarred
and enter another… One where the paper becomes my road, and
the pen becomes my vehicle. There have been times in my life where
I have put in many miles and this time has come once again. It is
time to unlock that safe that contains my innermost feelings, my
innermost feelings. I must say that again to myself. When I am in
this world, there is no one else but me and my tools and where I
go from there. My perspective, my reality, my perception, and my
point of view are directly correlated to my peace of mind and how
or whether I respect myself. Where I stand determines what I see.
Whether I have longevity or prosperity, or both or neither, is based
within that metaphorical safe that I speak of, and it needs to be
cleaned out. Insecurities, doubt, anger, rage, jealousy, frustration,
and impatience are all things that need to go. Until I have created
enough room for me to add the necessary ingredients to maintain
balance in my life, I will be lost in the land of the lost and lost
within my inner self."*

I felt like I could not escape the curses.

Deuteronomy chapter 28, verse 17:

"Cursed shall by thy basket an thy store."

After a short stay at Hazard projects, we went back home
to Adams Blvd. I remember that when we went back into
the house, the stereo and TV were gone. I figured that Pops
had "clucked" ("Clucked" is a hood term that means to sell
something for crack) them, like he did my Polaroid camera I
got in photography class. When smokers begin to cluck for
crack, it could be anything and they would be trying to sell
it. It could be a toaster for example that they would be trying

to get $5 bucks for. That $5 could get them a hit. When we got home, Pops was nowhere to be found.

Deuteronomy chapter 28, verse 18:

"Cursed shall be the fruit of thy body, and the fruit of thy land, the increase of thy kine, and the flock of thy sheep."

(A verse from a song I wrote "Where has the Love Gone?")

"Where has the love gone? I was raised by a Black man (De Franco Van Brocks "Pops") since my birth and even though his seed did not plant me on this earth, he gave me the strength that I needed. When he got smoked out, my heart bled. I look to God to ask why and when I did, I saw it in the skies and when it hit the ground. The smoke cleared all I saw was Black and Brown. Crack took the city by storm."

Deuteronomy chapter 28, verse 19:

"Cursed shalt thou be when thou comest in, and cursed shalt thou be when thou goes out."

(A verse from a song I wrote "Saturday Night")

"It's a Saturday night and the sun just set, snatched my keys and my wallet and straight jet. Kissed Moms goodbye and walked out the door. She wonders if I am gonna die on the concrete floor. I told Moms, "Don't worry, I'm just going around the corner. This is my hood. I ain't no foreigner." I walked through the car wash and said "what's up" to the homies I do not get sweated cause all the Gangstas know me. I cruised past the liquor store and kicked some change to the wino, he's just going to buy another bottle, yeah, I know. A jeep rolls by bumping some beat. I finally get to

the sign that says 28th Street. I pick my head up and stick my chest out. This is where I get my clout, where I get all my love from this town where all my peeps are Black and Brown... Like Rita and Maria, Altemecia and Kanesha. My brother said, "I got this girl that wants to meet ya." Now I'm headed for the end of a block. I passed the alley where the "Trekies" are smoking rock, the star trek fans say, "beam me up Scottie," as they inhale the fool's gold into their bodies. Finally, I reached my destination, and then I peep the situation that I'm facing. There's slapping of the bones on the table. Dank asks, "Are you ready?" when he knows I'm no good, but I am always willing and able. I pull the 40 from the brown paper bag and grabbed a seat; this is how it's done on 28th Street."

Deuteronomy chapter 28, verse 20:

"The LORD shall send upon thee cursing, vexation, and rebuke, in all that thou settest thine hand unto for to do, until thou be destroyed, and until thou perish quickly; because of the wickedness of thy doings, whereby thou hast forsaken me."

1987 was another Lakers championship year, that summer my mom took me downtown to see the parade. I was extremely excited! I had never seen so many people in one place in my short life span, since the 1984 Olympics. The backdrop of the scene was city hall, which was like the Empire State Building to me at that age. Seeing the sea of purple and gold, and hearing players like Erving "Magic" Johnson and James Worthy make their inspirational speeches, was surreal. The smell of street vendor's tacos and bacon wrapped hot dogs was intoxicating. I will never forget the deafening sound of the crowd after Coach Pat Riley guaranteed another trophy the following season! This was also the year that the Compton's entered our lives.

$\mathscr{C}$HAPTER 6

(1987) Boogie Down Productions released their debut album, "Criminal Minded." It focused more on the harsh realities of ghetto life, becoming an instant classic among hip-hop fans. Lead MC, KRS-ONE became an especially respected rapper among hip-hop's culture aficionados.

Public Enemy released their debut album, "Yo! Bum Rush the Show," on Def Jam. While it was praised by critics, it failed to make a similar impression on the charts.

'Push It,' a tune from Salt-N-Pepa's year-old album, "Hot, Cool & Vicious," was released nationally and ended up hitting number 19 on the pop charts and was nominated for a Grammy.

A former L.A. drug dealer named Eazy-E (Eric Wright) used his money to finance a small indie rap label called Ruthless Records. He signed a local group called H.B.O. and recruited Andre 'Dr. Dre' Young, who was a DJ/Producer from the R&B group World Class Wreckin' Cru, as well as Oshea Jackson, who was an up-and-coming MC who called himself Ice Cube.

Eric B. & Rakim released their debut album, "Paid In Full," which started hip-hop's love affair with James Brown samples. The emergence of Rakim introduced the dawning of the modern MC.

L.A. rapper, Ice-T, released his debut album, "Rhyme Pays," and became one of the first West Coast MCs to gain national attention. His single, 'Six In the Morning,' was groundbreaking with its harsh and explicit depiction of street hustling and criminal lifestyle.

MC Hammer, an Oakland-based dancer/rapper, released his debut album, "Let's Get It Started." It generated a few moderate hits, and Hammer gained attention for his exuberant dance moves and simple party raps.

Even before N.W.A., a Run D.M.C. show in Los Angeles ended in violence and Run DMC was blamed by the press for inciting the riot. The group called a press conference to defend itself and hip-hop was immediately thrust under a microscope by moral watchdogs and right-wing politicians.

One day, Moms came home with him, Rick Compton, and there they were at the front door. Moms said, "this is Rick" (Rick Compton Sr.) as he put his hand out to shake my hand, I just stood there and looked at him. Rick was average height, but a stout man in stature. He looked to be Caucasian with his blonde hair and blue eyes. But he had Latino styled gang tattoos, and one read "F13." That represented a long standing and notorious Mexican gang called "Florencia" (Florence). It was named after an infamous street in the South-Central part of Los Angeles. He had another "tat" (short for tattoo) that read "Musky," which was his gang name. That is when I figured out how we were able to come home, and why Pops was gone. Rick must have come and kicked

Pops and his crackhead homies out of the house so we could come home. As a matter of fact, I remember being woke up one night shortly after we came home, I heard some tussling downstairs. All I can remember was seeing from the top of the stairs, Pops' feet were pointed horizontally which meant he was laid out on the floor. Rick was standing over him and yelling about Pops stealing some of his dress shoes. Come to find out, Rick and Moms worked together. I remember seeing him at Hazard projects, but I thought it was just work related as I saw him talking to some gang bangers from "Big Hazard." I remember seeing the decal on the side of the car CYGS (Community Youth Gang Services). I was finally told by my mother that her and Rick worked together, even though I had figured out that their relationship was more than that. This was either a non-profit or city program that worked closely with and was a liaison between city police departments and local city gangs. If I am not mistaken, you had to be an ex-gang member to work there. You can imagine my surprise when I found that out, (since I had never known) that my mother was an ex-gang member. There were some stories my mom told me about her job that described just how difficult it was. Having to inform family members of gang related deaths/murders or helping to avoid other deaths by the way of coordinating truce events and how they were sometimes targeted by gang members who did not appreciate their efforts as it interfered with drug/blood money being made. There was a rumor that one of Moms' co-workers had given too much inside info, to the makers of the movie "American Me" that was about the beginnings of the Mexican Mafia "La Eme." I heard rumors that she was executed.

Silas said regarding Rick, "I could tell he was a real selfish person, because he was in it for Dolores and not for her kids. I knew that he didn't care, and I knew it wasn't going to be productive for me, so I knew I had to get out of that situation as soon as possible."

Deuteronomy chapter 28, verse 21:

"The LORD shall make the pestilence cleave unto thee, until he have consumed thee from off the land, whither thou goest to possess it."

Later, Rick would bring his oldest son Ricky Lee Compton Jr. to the house. Ricky's story is one of desperation and despair from the beginning. His mother, according to him, was a drug addict. He told us of stories when he had to go to the local grocery store, where he would carry bags to cars for a quarter. He said he had to help support his little brother as it was just them and their mother. He eventually went to live with his grandmother on his mom's side. From there is how he made it to us and ended up running away a few times and was gone for months at a time. Ricky became a member of the extended family, even though he wasn't around on a consistent basis. He was still deemed to be one of the "Young Prophets" of the Movement. He wrote and recorded and performed with us (when he was there to do so) and my brother is talented. Ricky did contribute, when he was around, but it just seemed that whenever it got hot; he had to leave the kitchen. He was forged in the fires of drug and gang life (even though he did not bang, he would later get caught up on drugs) He bounced around from a young age, from spot to spot, and just never would stick anywhere. When he came to live with us on Adams, he ended up running away more than once. (a pattern he developed through his life) Whether it was the scuffles with our brothers Silas and Josiah (he was closer to their age than mine) or whether it was the problem he had with his father's forms of discipline. Rick Sr. would either beat his son or make him write standards or both. For those of you who don't know what standards are, teachers used to make students do them as a form of discipline. They would make you write one sentence, hundreds of times. The sentence had something to do with whatever you did wrong.

Ricky at one point became a ward of the state and was placed in a group home. He eventually ran away from there and made his way back to the Movement as he always has. He ended up making his way up to Washington state, to live with his mother. He found out his mother had cancer, and he went to take care of her as well as it was another opportunity for him to run away from whatever current circumstances, he was not comfortable with or could not handle at that time. He made his way back down to LA for his father's funeral, who had lost his own battle with drugs and mental and physical health issues. Ricky went back up to Washington to be with his mother who ended up passing herself some months later. The whole time he was in the fight of his life, fighting the devil, the drugs and himself. He like the rest of us continues to battle his inner demons to this day.

Deuteronomy chapter 28, verse 22: *"The LORD shall smite thee with a consumption, and with a fever, and with an inflammation, and with an extreme burning, and with the sword, and with blasting, and with mildew; and they shall pursue thee until thou perish."*

1988 brought us the "Back 2 Back" Laker championship that Pat Riley guaranteed, and it would be the last in the "Showtime" era. We would go on a twelve-year drought before we saw another in the form of Shaq & Kobe in the 1999-2000 season. The Dodgers also won the world series that year and I will never forget witnessing Kirk Gibson stepping to the plate as a DH (designated hitter) with a bum wheel (leg) and hitting that walk-off homer and rounding the bases pumping his fists the whole trip around. The Dodgers have not won another until 2020. 1988 had its ups and downs like any other year, especially at the influential age of sixteen. I had fell in love for the first time, had a lot going on at home, and school was getting harder. I know at one point that year I had thought about suicide (for about 10 seconds) I remember thinking how much I loved myself and life too much. The highlight of that year was being selected for YCC (Youth Conservation Corps) in Yosemite for that summer.

CHAPTER 7

(1988) Erick Sermon and Parish Smith, collectively known as EPMD, released their debut album, "Strictly Business." The pair became one of the most celebrated duos in hip-hop underground and shunned the spotlight in the wake of commercial Rap's exploding popularity.

As Boogie Down Productions began production on their second album, DJ Scott La Rock was gunned down following an altercation. Stunned by the sudden death of his partner, KRS-One carried on and evolved into 'The Teacha,' who promoted a more educated and socially aware approach to hardcore hip-hop. KRS calls it "Edutainment," education through entertainment.

MC Lyte; a brash, young 'female' MC, became the first female hardcore rapper signed to a major label and released her debut album, "Lyte As A Rock."

Public Enemy released their second album, "It Takes A Nation of Millions to Hold Us Back." With its use of dense, layered sampling and hard funk, their politically incited rhymes were hailed by rap and rock critics alike. Public Enemy's popularity skyrocketed.

Ice-T's second album, "Power," became the first rap album to carry a Parental Advisory warning label.

The Birth of a Movement

Afrika Bambaataa formed the Native Tongues crew, after hearing an underground single called "Wrath of My Madness," recruited a young female MC from New Jersey named Queen Latifah.

N.W.A. released their debut album, "Straight Outta Compton." Taking the hardcore attack of Public Enemy and merging it with brutally explicit tales of the crime-ridden streets of South-Central Los Angeles, it became a historic moment for 'gangsta rap' and for West Coast rappers to gain national attention.

N. W.A.'s song, 'Fuck the Police,' incited mega controversy over its lyrics and led the F.B.I. to issue a formal warning to the group, Ruthless Records, and its parent-label, Priority. This also started a long-standing battle between the powers-that-be and gangsta rap.

A trio of friends from Harlem NY, the Jungle Brothers, released their debut album, 'Straight Out The Jungle' on the small Idler label. The album didn't gain much attention. It did however provide a new take on hip-hop that was neither 'gangsta' nor overly political. They joined up with Afrika Bambaataa's "Native Tongues'" crew, and incorporated elements of jazz, house music and used Afrocentric themes. The Jungles Brothers introduce a new subgenre that would later be called 'alternative' rap.

It was the summer of 88 and I was in the majestic mountains of Yosemite National Park (California). This is where I wrote my first poem, before all the works you have read thus far. It was raining that afternoon and I was sitting under a tarp, on a rock, next to a waterfall as I wrote it. At that age, I could not fully fathom the impact of that environment.

Stripped down to its essentials, the earth exposed, and its truth revealed. I remember the scene like something out of a movie; I remember thinking how cliché' this would read. It all fell into place in that moment and when I think about the overwhelming feeling of being in the presence of God's masterpiece, to this day I get lost in my own thoughts If you have never seen so much as a picture of Yosemite or its surrounding areas, you are missing some of the things that make life worth living and that are a perfect example of the duality of simplicity and complexity in all living things. Twenty-five miles in the "back country" (God's land, civilization nowhere to be found, only nature) is where you can travel back in time to experience what it was like before the industrial revolution and is the closest, I have ever gotten to my ancestors. (Cherokee) The Yosemite Valley, El Capitan, Half Dome, The Meadows, Mt. Dana and the neighboring Sequoia National Forest are all encompassing.

(My first poem)

"Alone, never alone yet always. Surrounded by thousands and still alone. Alone, never alone yet always. Usually away from the crowd, wanting them to recognize, wanting them to realize, yet you stay alone. Alone, never alone yet always. Conceived by two and sometimes one until you grow to know the meaning of alone. Wanting and waiting for something new. My God and Lord, his ring and sword. Never will the skies stay blue, sing our song as life moves along and never forget we're always alone."

Before this poem, I knew of my gift for writing, it was the gift of this poem that gave me the realization that since the inception of our entities, we have and will be alone. Since the moment, God gave us our own souls, we have and will be alone. And so, began my journey with God, nature, my thoughts, and feelings.

I was chosen from my school to represent the Southern California region for Y.C.C (Youth Conservation Corps) summer program in Yosemite. There were thirty kids, three groups of ten, from across the United States that were selected to participate. This was a junior version of the C.C.C. (California Conservation Corps) who did everything we did on a grander scale and including forest fire fighting efforts. It was extremely hard and physical work; I was fifteen and up for the challenge. I had only really been to one other summer camp when I was younger. I believe it was called "Camp Pyles." I remember what they called "survival week," when our cabin/group was kicked out of the main camp and only given the essentials regarding food, tarps and gear needed to survive in the wilderness for a week. There were four cabins/groups, and the objective was to see if we could survive without having to return to the main camp for that week and to bring back with us the lessons that week had taught us. I remember one night it rained as if we were in a tropical monsoon and all we had for shelter was an individual tarp and sleeping bag. One of the boys from our group injured himself on a day hike. I think he broke an ankle or leg and two of us were sent back to the main camp to retrieve help. (Would become a recurring theme.) It was my self and another boy who ran like the winds of "Hurricane Katrina" in our youth, to call for reinforcements. They had to land a helicopter in a nearby clearing to air lift the boy to a hospital, miles away. We were treated like heroes! I think the camp was located somewhere in between Fresno and the bay area in northern California and we had to hike ten miles inland to reach it. It was an invaluable experience but was only slightly and in the least did it prepare me for the work that was to come in Yosemite.

In Yosemite, we did things like build trails where there were none. We would build and create irrigation systems where they were needed. We built bear boxes for campers in the Valley to keep their food from bears. We put up barbwire fences (just off main roads) to keep animals from crossing those roads and getting killed and causing car accidents. We went to remote and secluded areas to re-plant almost extinct vegetation. We also helped with forest fire fighting efforts. Some of these jobs required hiking to and from the work sites, about ten miles a day while wearing 100lbs. back packs and carrying our tools. I learned so much and was able to develop as a young person. My development was recognized as I was asked back the following summer to be part of the staff.

We played just as hard as we worked and on weekends, instead of resting, we went white water rafting or hiking up fourteen-thousand-foot mountain peaks. There was a weekend we were white water rafting, and I ended up getting a cut on the bottom of my foot that threatened my staying in the program for the rest of that summer. If I were not able to continue to perform at the same level I had been, I would have been sent home. I was somehow able to do it. But I do remember the week we were working on the barbwire fence project, there was a terrible accident with one of my fellow team members. The barbwire was in spindles and had to be unwrapped and wrapped around the posts using a tool that pulled it and created tension in the barbwire. This ensured the fence was tight and would hold. So, one of my team members who happened to be a female (not that it mattered, just a fact) when cutting the barbwire, did not follow protocol and it snapped back and hit her in the face. They thought it was in the eye because blood was gushing everywhere, and she could not see. I ran with a limp for 5 miles back to our vehicle to gather the first aid kit and radio and ran 5 miles back to the work site. Come to find out that the barbwire only hit the bridge of her nose but punctured a blood vessel that led her and everybody else to believe it was her eye. My foot eventually healed, and I was able to stay for the rest of the summer, thanks to my youth and quick healing ability. The lessons I learned those summers in Yosemite were invaluable and have stuck with me to this day. The teamwork and leadership it took to accomplish the missions successfully on a day-to-day basis, cannot be overlooked or understated. The preparation that was needed and the discipline it took to follow through, gave way to whatever you thought you knew. It was all new and there was absolutely no way to fake it until you made it. The time frame was only six months of my life, but the memories and direction given have and I believe will last my lifetime.

Deuteronomy chapter 28, verse 23:

"And thy heaven that is over thy head shall be brass, and the earth that is under thee shall be iron."

At this point in my life, I feel like I can survive anything and anywhere, whether it be the wilderness or the streets. Unfortunately, they seem to have quite a few similarities, as they can both be very calloused and unforgiving. I was blessed to be in Yosemite that summer and the next for more than one reason. I was blessed to be there and not home for the summer.

Home was the West Adams Historical District of Los Angeles, where "Sugar" Ray Robinson (legendary boxer, before Sugar Ray Leonard) lived on the corner of Adams Blvd. and Edgehill Dr., we knew his son Chuck. He was older than us and always stopped to talk to us whenever he walked through the block and always dropped pearls of wisdom on us as youngsters. For years, the West Adams Avenue Jazz Festival took place on Adams, just off 7th Avenue. The most important years of my life were spent on the block of 28th Street, the next block south of Adams Boulevard. Home was hot in the summer and not because of the weather. The heat was from the streets, from the bullets that have no eyes in the chambers of those steel handheld dragons that spit fire and nails into the coffins of those in its path.

Deuteronomy chapter 28, verse 24:

"The LORD shall make rain of thy land powder and dust: from heaven shall it come down upon thee, until thou be destroyed."

(A verse from a song I wrote)

"We used to chill on the top of the hill with the steel, dealing with no hassles on the porch of the castle as we wrestled with thoughts of Watts and the truce, red and blue. We are just some black and brown dogs from the deuce eight block. We didn't carry Glocks; we used to carry Mac–10's, Mexicans and Africans. Who is the original indigenous man of this land? I am the lighter whiter shade, wondering why we haven't made it yet.

Revolution is the solution, and I would bet my life on it, and we would die to represent!"

Deuteronomy chapter 28, verse 25:

"The LORD shall cause thee to be smitten before thine enemies: thou shalt go out one way against them, and flee seven ways before them: and shalt be removed into all the kingdoms of the earth."

These were rough times for me, I was seventeen and gearing up for my senior year of high school. I was ready to graduate, go to college and get out of the hood. We grew up poor and I was used to it by then, but it did not make it any easier to deal with. It was harder as you got older and as those peers at school or in the neighborhood would notice more and be more vocal about it. Kids, teens, and young adults could be extremely mean and cold hearted when it came to the competition of materialism. Who has more than who and whose is better? (Shoes, clothes, jewelry, electronics) It was funny though, cause most of these kids were coming from a same place, both geographically as well as financially. Maybe some had both parents and maybe not, but maybe their single parents had a little bit better job. Maybe their parents were teased and made it a point to make sure their kids would not be, even if that meant breaking their bank accounts or wallets. I got paid from the summer before at Yosemite and still had some money left over, but there was more than that going on and whenever there were rough times, I would write. I remember writing about this, the time of the teachers' strike of 1989.

$\mathcal{C}$HAPTER 8

(1989) *Public Enemy released their much-anticipated third album, "Fear of A Black Planet." (Was officially released April 10, 1990) They were awarded strong sales and reviews, despite controversy over anti-Semitic remarks made by group member Professor Griff in an interview. Chuck D formally dismissed Griff from the group.*

The Grammy committee announced that rap would be given its own official Grammy category. The news was great; however, it was later announced that the presentation would not be televised. As a result, most of the prominent artists of that era, including Salt-N-Pepa, Public Enemy, DJ Jazzy Jeff & the Fresh Prince, Ice-T and more, hosted a "Boycott the Grammys Party" on MTV the night of the broadcast. DJ Jazzy Jeff & the Fresh Prince went on to win the award.

After a year of buzz swirling around her underground singles, Queen Latifah released her debut album, "All Hail the Queen." It was praised profusely by the hip-hop community for its positive lyrics and strong feminist overtones.

To squash the surge of Black-On-Black crime in New York and as a tribute to Scott La Rock, KRS-ONE organized the "Stop the Violence Movement" with several New York rappers. Soon, the

Movement went national, and the West Coast MCs got involved. The result was two public-service singles denouncing violence, 'Self Destruction' in New York, and 'We're All in the Same Gang' in Los Angeles.

Doug E. Fresh's former partner, MC Ricky D who started calling himself 'Slick Rick' released his solo debut, "The Great Adventures of Slick Rick" on Def Jam Records. With laid-back rhymes and vivid storytelling, Rick is immediately elevated to the top-tier of MCs.

Ice Cube announced his leaving of the group N.W.A. after a financial dispute with Eazy-E and manager, Jerry Heller.

De La Soul, a young rap group from Long Island, New York who was also affiliated with the Native Tongues collective, released their debut, "3 Feet High & Rising" on Tommy Boy Records. Displaying quirky samples from rock, funk, folk, country and soul and illuminating wordplay ranging from psychedelic themes to straight out gibberish, the group was immediately called the future of hip-hop music.

MC Hammer released his sophomore album, "Please Hammer, Don't Hurt 'Em." The album was ripped by critics and laughed at by hip-hop purists but became a huge hit.

Sparked by the wildly popular single, 'U Can't Touch This,' and heavy video rotation on MTV, the album sold ten million copies and with his flashy dancing and trademark baggy pants, MC Hammer became an international superstar.

2 Live Crew, a Florida based party themed rap group, released their third album, "As Nasty As They Wanna Be." It was extremely explicit and sexually provocative, with lyrics reaching near-pornographic proportions and was banned from sale in the state of

Florida. The group themselves were arrested for lewdness after performing a concert in Miami. The group went to court for their right to perform and write music as they wanted to, the group was found not guilty in what became a heated debate over decency and the First Amendment.

Rick Rubin left Def Jam and formed a new label, "Def American."

Yo! MTV Raps made its debut, with host Fab 5 Freddy. For the first time, the entire country had a platform to watch the latest music videos by all the top rap artists.

I went to Mid-City Alternative, a magnet school. It was a K-12 school (Kindergarten through twelfth grade) It was a school of alternative education, for example, on Fridays we did not have traditional academics. We would instead go on field trips. One semester I took sailing, and every Friday we went to San Pedro Harbor, where one of my teachers had a sailboat. He would teach us how to sail and one of the semesters we got the opportunity to sail to Catalina Island. At the end of the school year, we were blessed to go to camping for a week; Marques (whose story will come a little later) used to call it a "Camp Snoopy" (comparing it to the kids' section at Knott's Berry Farm).

It was a public school, magnet school, which meant the inner-city east side (the worst part of the city in terms of poverty and crime) kids were bused in. Eventually and unfortunately, this became one of the reasons that the experimental education was not successful at this school. It was a shame since those were the kids that needed it most and due to many different factors, were not able to take advantage of it. I started there in fifth grade and as it came to junior high (now called Middle School), the curriculum became more independent. The students were given the opportunity to choose their schedules if they met their class requirements for that grade. This and the fact that it was an open campus proved to be too much independence for most of the students to handle.

Before going to Mid-City, I do remember going to 6th Avenue Elementary School for the fourth grade. The only prominent and dominant memory I have from that experience was the fact that the school bully, who happened to be a girl (a cute girl too) chose me to be her boyfriend (I did not have a choice in the matter). This meant I had protection for the year and a cute girlfriend to boot.

I believe that when they found two seniors having sex in independent French class at Mid-City and students gambling in the parking lot, they figured that it was not working as they had planned. I remember participating in the gambling, we played "Pitching Pennies" (where two people stood behind a line and threw coins towards a wall, whoever landed their coin closest to the wall, took both coins) and "Big Bank take Lil Bank" (this was where two people decided to play based on the thought process that they had more money in their pocket than the person they were playing with. If they were right, they took the other person's money and if not, the other person took their money).

The illegal activities aside, this was where I was supposed to be. It was perfect for me, being the oldest of five and being given so much responsibility at an early age. Both directly and indirectly, it made independence a good thing for me. I remember discovering my blessing for writing first in the seventh grade; between short stories, poetry, and creative writing, I fell in love with the art form. The appreciation of course came as I realized the escape I received from reading, the escape and release were even more intense when I wrote. I love to read and when I write, I read what I write as I write it. I remember loving school and I remember loving to learn. I remember that when there were problems at home, I would lose myself in school. I remember starting to wonder and to think about going to college and whether I would measure up. I had to ask myself if I would be college material and decided to write a book of that title.

"College Material"

May 15, 1989 was the second teachers' strike in the history of L.A.U.S.D (Los Angeles Unified School District), the only one I have experienced in all the eleven years of my education. I have never seen anything like it. The first day was calm, not much to report. Second day, no sign of letting up as the teachers push forth their message. Chaos begins to break out.

(Seventh grade English descriptive paper, based on a picture of a fox with a rabbit in his mouth)

"As I walked along the cold white snowflakes, I tried to catch my breath. This rabbit was no easy creature to catch. What a struggle he gave me; I must rest. Looking around at these hills, which are covered with rocks and dead dried up a grass, I am chilled. The wind whistles by and rustles my brown coat of fur. The winter hills look dead but are livened up easily by a white blanket of snow. How I wish it were summer again, I would not need fur in the summer. That big bright shining star warns me like a giant heater. I can be lazy, just lie around all day with no need for shelter. It is not, it's not summer, it is winter, cold, and dark and long winter. There is a great need for shelter and just like myself, all animals run and fight for shelter, especially at the beginning of winter, I am glad I found shelter. I cannot wait to get back to my hole. I will eat what I have caught, then sleep. Taking one last breath of crisp winter air, I prepare for the long journey home."

It was my first year of real creative thinking and my first taste of real commercial literature. Right away it appealed to me. The reason for this was my first English teacher, his appearance was sturdy as he was a short, stocky, and grey bearded. He taught junior high, seventh to ninth grades and was very strict. Going to an alternative school had its advantages and disadvantages like any other school. At this school, which I attended since the fifth grade, things were different. You see, around fifth and sixth grades were when the warnings began, "Damn Franco, wait till you get Pat." At our school, teachers went by their first names, as this was part of an alternative education. There was Mike, a math teacher who was the school bank. He loaned students money to teach them responsibility and money management. He was a tall and burly man with a long gray and white beard, RIP Mike, he passed away some years back. There was Joel, a history and social studies teacher. He was one of the coolest and used to pull out a TV in class often. He liked to teach visually, and I remember in 1988 when the Dodgers were in the world series, and he let us watch part of a day game. There was Jim, a science teacher who was our resident sailing instructor. He lived on his sailboat in the San Pedro harbor. There was Doc, who was an AP (Advanced Placement) English teacher and our basketball coach. Doc taught on the high school level, another of the best ones. He was funny and strict, and you had better not think you were going to take advantage of him because he was in a wheelchair. By the time seventh grade came around, you could imagine what I anticipated but...

Third day - As I do every day, I turned on the 4:00 PM news.

Progress being made, negotiations around the clock, new proposal by teachers brings surplus money from Sacramento. Things looking good! One-third of L.A.U.S. D's students out of school, ditching, LAPD lends a hand with the rounding up of students. Chaos somewhat under control, things looking OK.

The rumors were nothing but that, rumors. He was a good teacher, to me anyway. I learned a lot from him and about him, he also learned about me. He saw my capability and potential and he brought the best out of me.

(Eighth grade English essay)

"While I sit here thinking of what I am going to write, I notice how dim this room is. I cannot figure it out. On one hand it takes on a tiny kitchen look, but on the other I can see a little washroom. It is full of typewriters and there is a sink with a somewhat tinted

window above it. The sink is aged and filled with dust. Hooked to the wall next to the sink is a paper towel dispenser and next to that is a soap container. This room is almost office like, no more of a kitchen type. Above the door there is a long light fixture, looks like one of those from a classroom or an office building. To the side of the light there are a bunch of pipes, they look like gas pipes. The room is painted a drab, yellowish color, the cabinets are barely noticeable and seem to be empty except for a few cobwebs and a couple of bowls. There are a few chairs and a few boxes on the floor along with a lot of trash. Under the sink are a few more cabinets and along the sink is a sort of L shaped counter, on this counter there are some more typewriters, an old scrub brush and a worn-out sponge. In a corner there is a big old fashioned vacuum cleaner. It looks like a giant lawnmower! This room makes me feel ancient and (I do not know I guess it is my imagination) but I still wonder how all the stuff got here. What was this room used for? I guess I will never know…in the meantime, I think I got something!

The sun rises from its place, peers through my white curtains and across my face. And so, my day begins.

Eighth grade, Pat was still my English teacher. As an elective I thought I would take typing. So, on that cloudy day, I sat in that room, and it was just me and the typewriter. I talked to her, and she talked to me, and we established a relationship that I hope will last for years to come.

Fourth day - U.T.L.A (United Teachers of L.A). representatives met with board of education administrative representatives for the first time in one hundred twenty days. Good news or bad? Ninth grade was tough for me, education wise. I was having a lot of home problems and at the same time, I was falling in love. Of course, this affected my grades at school. This was the first year I was introduced to and familiarized with letter grades. The previous two grades or years, I was receiving credit or no credit. Before that I was getting straight A's. The pressures of higher education levels, letter grades and home life, began to become too hot to handle. I struggled all year and was able to pull out the worst grades of my life, two C's and a D. The family problems consisted of parent separation, turning me into the man of the house. Father was fighting the separation and I mean literally fighting. Not to mention drug abuse in the house, causing my mother to turn to alcohol. During this time, I became a father figure as well as a big brother. I had two little brothers and one little sister at the time, which I helped raise for a while. I did my best with them and did what I could to help my mother. The problems with my father, within our family, went back a lot further.

I never finished that book, "College Material," and maybe someday I will. For now, I must finish this one. I graduated high school in 1990, out of a class of twenty. I was valedictorian and student athlete of that year. I was the only one in my class that was going directly to a four-year university. It seemed that I was missing a semester of a foreign language. I remembered meeting with my Spanish teacher and him asking me what grade I thought I deserved. I also remember saying to him that I thought a B would be fair. I did not take that semester of Spanish, but I did finish with the requirements needed to graduate with a 3.7 GPA. I took the SAT test and got the score I needed and applied to some universities out of state for which I was accepted. After long thought and consideration, I settled on HSU (Humboldt State University) which was as far away from the hood I could get and still be within the state and not have to pay out-of-state fees.

$\mathcal{C}$HAPTER 9

(1990) Return of the B-Boy in the UK. B-Boys were back. There was massive interest in the dance form within British Hip-Hop culture. The revival there was led by crews such as Born To Rock, UK Rock Steady Crew and Second To None. The "DJ Stretch Armstrong and Bobbito Show" launched from 1990 to 1998 on WKCR 89.9FM in NY 2Pac joined Digital Underground as a roadie and dancer. Schoolly D appeared on the Phil Donahue Show to talk about 'Money & Rap music'.

As you can see, all these events in my life are intertwined and made up the most important times and moments in my life. They were the steppingstones and foundational building blocks that have made me the person I am today.

This time and these events were a prelude to an even more important future. A small group of kids, growing up in the same neighborhood in South Central Los Angeles, met on this street known as 28th Street. At the top of the hill resided the Jones family, Connie "Moms" only Casey at the time, Marques.

Jones (Big Bro), and my childhood crush (now wife) Nikki Jones.

I know I have mentioned him, and now it is time to let you know who Marques was and is to me and tell some of his story. Marques is the son of Connie, big brother to Nikki and his half-sister Nicole and half-brother Joey (RIP, he died some years back at thirty-four, from complications with Type 1 Diabetes), who both have different mothers. His father, also named Marques was not around mostly, while he grew up. His Father, brother Joey and sister Nicole were in and out of his life growing up. He loved his brother and cherished the time they did spend together when they were young. As they got older, they grew apart in space and in their personalities. They did not get along when they were around each other, later in life. But when Joey ended up in the hospital in Las Vegas (where he lived at the time) Marques, Nikki and I made our way down there as fast as we could get there. Marques was upset with Joey for not taking care of himself and they argued. Joey had Diabetes and he wasn't taking it seriously; he wasn't watching what he ate nor taking his medicine. He ended up in the hospital a couple of times before he passed. I think his attitude was that he wasn't going to let his disease dictate his life. He ate what he wanted, he drank and didn't take his medicine. Joey's death hit Marques hard, especially since he had attempted to contact him just before his death. He wanted to reconcile their estranged relationship and did not get the chance.

Deuteronomy chapter 28, verse 26:

"And thy carcase shall be meat unto all fowls of the air, and unto the beasts if the earth, and no man shall fray them away."

He grew up with his mother Connie and his sister Nikki. He, like myself, are the eldest of our siblings. This is one of our similarities, yet there are way more differences. From the time we met on 28th Street, we didn't like each other, at all. I thought he was an arrogant, loudmouth Asshole! And I was just this white boy that just showed up on his block. It is ironic how we went from that point to becoming the brothers we are today. Like I said, there are more differences than similarities, we are complete opposites. That is how we balance each other out, like Yin and Yang. What I lacked, he had and vice versa. Without too many positive male figures to look up to, we helped each other grow up.

He met and knew the Barrigas before me and when I met them at Mid-City Alternative, found out they only lived on the other block over from where I lived. When I started coming on the block, he was always around. I was tightest with Carlos "Los" Barriga and Marques was best friends with Jesus "Chuey" Barriga and tighter with Luis "Mixer" Barriga. Carlos was the joker of the bunch; Luis was more mischievous, and I think that is why Marques gravitated toward him more. They both liked to talk a lot of shit too. Marques tells a story, "I was always with Chuey and I didn't really kick it with Mixer until one night, we walked to the store down the hill and we smoked a joint. We got the munchies, and I got some Laura Scudder's BBQ chips. While we were gone, Carlos snitched and when we got back, Jesus was waiting on us. He started grilling me and asked, "Did you smoke weed with Luis Alberto?" (Alberto is Luis' middle name and any time Latinos include the middle name, it usually means someone is in trouble) He said that Carlos told him that we were smoking weed and I told Chuey that I was smoking weed, not Luis. But we were both high as FUCK!" Marques chuckles.

We used to hang out a lot in the Barriga's back yard or in their house, where we were always welcomed and always fed well. Even though I crushed hard on Marques' sister Nikki when I first laid eyes on her, it was Margarita "Maggie" Barriga who was my first love. It was Jr. High when I fell in love with her. We would sit on her front porch and listen to "Oldies" from a boom box (portable radio) and watch the stars. I was on 28th Street more and more as I got older until it was every day. We were the crew and were always together, we did everything together.

I remember the first time I went to Marques' house. Carlos and I went up to meet Marques, I think we were about to get him because we were about to go somewhere, and he was always late. I think it's a Jones trait, cause Connie, him and Nikki all have the trait. So, when we finally got up the stairs and into the house and into his room, I was blown away. He had a lot of clothes, shoes, and colognes. He was still getting ready, and Carlos was trying to steal some of his cologne. Marques smacked his hand and said, "Don't touch that one, here you can have some of this one," as he continued to talk shit about Carlos touching his stuff.

Marques' family didn't have a lot of money, Connie was a single working mother, yet Marques liked expensive and good things and he found a way to get them on his own. I later found out; it was mostly from hustling. Marques did work a few jobs throughout his life yet gravitated more towards hustling. When I came back from college, I joined him.

The Jones' lived in the "castle at the top of the hill," on 28th Street, that is what we called it. I think at one point somebody counted the stairs and I believe the count was fifty-three. It was a winding staircase, and the architecture of the building took on the decorum of a castle. Directly across the street lived Mrs. Smith an elderly woman whose son committed suicide in the garage. She was a nice lady, but she was also "Neighborhood watch."

Next door, on the same side of the block, lived the Barriga family. Padre y Madre (father and mother), five boys and five girls all lived in one three-bedroom house. There was a son-in-law and a daughter-in-law which calculated to three separate families. Over some years they have added four more rooms in the back of the house. On the Jones side of the block, a few apartment complexes down, lived the Williams family. Mother and son Avery who was part of the crew, but more part of the block. He was an only child and went to a private school, where he played basketball. We played ball with Avery when we could and when he was around. Sports were always a big part of our lives, from playing football and baseball in the street, to basketball in the back yard. We used to play b-ball at Mt. Vernon jr. high, hoover park, LA Trade Tech College, UCLA, Overland Park, and pretty much anywhere we could. We were competitive and had the mentality that is was our team against the world. I played organized soccer, football, and basketball. Marques played organized baseball at Pan Pacific Park. We learned from sports, like how to work with a team and play your part. We learned discipline and respect. We learned that the games are 80% mental and 20%

physical. There were so many lessons learned in sports that later in life we ended up coaching football in Snoop Dogg's youth football league.

There was also Jovan and Ian, who also lived in Avery's building with their mother. Jovan later became a member of the Easy Riders and is serving a life sentence for murder. Ian popped in and out of the circle over the years and it has been years since we last seen him. This was 28th Street, also known as the "deuce eight block. "

Marques talked about first touching down in the neighborhood and his first trip down the block, "I remember that first day walking down the block with my cousin, we were going to the store and you guys were playing in the street. You guys were playing baseball and Melvin got ran over by that guy on the ten-speed and me and my cousin were laughing, and you guys were looking at us like you wanted to fight. I was like "what nigga what?" I was the new nigga on the block." And about the Barrigas, Marques said, "Man that's my family and they will be my familia forever. They are my Mexican family and without them things might have gone bad for me. They were there for me and that's emotional cause I would die for them, and I know they would die for me. There was an example when my dad was abusing me and the whole familia (family) came outside with their cueatas (guns) getting ready to blast my dad away. But, by me honoring my father, I stopped them from acting and from that day alone an unconditional love was set in my heart that will never die. There was another time when the "scraps" (a local enemy gang to BPS) tried to get me when I was walking up the street and

I had to make a dash up the side of an apartment building. I wasn't even gang banging and had to find safety for my life. I didn't even know the eldest son/brother Chavo. Chavo saw me across the street sitting on my stairs and he knew I was hot and wanted to kill niggas! He gave me a 20-gauge shotgun and some shells and told me I could hold it as long as I needed it. When I was shot up and, in the hospital, and my mom (Connie) had to go to work so she wouldn't lose her job, I remember waking up and momma Maria was there. I learned Spanish just to communicate with her. They were an inspiration in my life, and it was all love, Black and Brown love before I knew about it."

At the bottom of the hill was the street that intersects 28 th Street, Montclair. Now Montclair has been infamous for years, mostly for drugs and violence. Marques called it, "The block that was always hot! Whether it was the pop, pop, pop!!! Or it was the weed, pills or crack rock on the spot!" On the corner of 28th street and Montclair was L.A.'s cleaners (LA was an older Black gentleman, native to those parts) and next to the cleaners was the motorcycle club. I learned how to play and shark at pool there as a kid. Across the street from the cleaners, on the other corner was Dave's liquor store. The first owner of this liquor store was shot and killed in the doorway, with his pistol in hand. Dave was a Middle Eastern man who also earned the respect of the neighborhood in a few years. On the same side of the street as Dave's was Chuck's barber shop/neighborhood hangout. On the same side of Montclair down from the cleaners, was Tanner's market. Tanners was owned by a Korean family and the father's name was Mr. C. I spent a lot of my childhood in that liquor store/market, between the video games like "Mario Bros." and "Gallaga" to the goodies like "Now & Laters" and "Icees." Silas talked about, "going to Tanner's Market around the young age of 8 or 9 by myself and going there with my mom's cigarette note, making sure she got her cigarettes and picking up some candy for myself at the same time." And on the corner of Montclair and Adams Boulevard was the car wash. That was the makeup of Montclair. It was all the intricacies within that street and the neighborhood that made it what it was. Silas called it, "a city within a city, it was a hub where a community got together." It wasn't pretty, but it was home, and it felt like family, and it was the village. (Dysfunctional village) Montclair looked like Chicago (B.P.S. Black P Stone was a gang from Chicago) in ways and had a different feel to it than being a block in L.A. It was like its own city. Montclair was the backdrop to Hollywood and provided the entertainment industry with plenty of scenes for movies such as "Bullworth" as well as music videos and documentaries. Other movies such as "White Men can't Jump" and "Boyz N the Hood" were filmed in the local areas such as on Crenshaw, in and around Baldwin Hills and in the "Jungles."

Deuteronomy chapter 28, verse 27:

"The LORD will smite thee with the botch of Egypt, and with the emerods, and with the scab, and with the itch, whereof thou canst not be healed."

The Latin/"Cholo" gang of the neighborhood was "Easy Riders" and most of the time they got along with BPS as they had to, being surrounded by enemy gangs on all sides. I remember when I was young, and the gang bangers hung out at the car wash next door to my apartment building on Adams Blvd. When I walked through the car wash, I always got love from the O.G.'s, but when I was young and the younger gang members (Baby G's) used to mess with me. The OG's would tell them to leave me alone and give me a "pass," because I went to school and got good grades.

(A verse from The Black and Brown Movement song, "Ghetto Winds")

"Swinging in the mist of these Ghetto Winds; wishing amends for our enemies and our friends. When will this crime and this murder end? While we are swaying in the mist of these Ghetto Winds… Every day that passes, feels like I'm getting older. Just some more stress, some more weight on my shoulders. Strain on my brain…every night I pray to regain my senses; then I cleanse my lenses. That way I can see clearly, at times we nearly falling… why the FUCK does everybody think that we are balling? We stand tall when we are calling on our Lord for the strength to go the length and the distance. In an instance, our peoples be flipping like a light switch, off and on they be switching. It's on our arms for life, we trust no bitch. Now, a bitch can either be a female or a male…it's just a simple case of show and tell. If you have no soul, it's your soul you sell and if you're not standing, you've already fell. So, tell me how deep the well is, when you're swinging in the mist of the ghetto winds."

Deuteronomy chapter 28, verse 28:

"The LORD shall smite thee with madness, and blindness, and astonishment of the heart:"

Like most neighborhoods of South Central, the Eastside, the Westside, East LA, and West Adams (off Crenshaw) there were "gang bangers" and "dope slangers," there was death and destruction, life and love and the pursuit of happiness. Most of all there was a lot of surviving and just getting by. Therefore, I always looked at it as a blessing for me not to be in the hood during those summers I was able to get away. That summer heat always seemed to bring out the worse in some, as if the heat waves that can be seen rising from the horizon of a concrete sidewalk or asphalt street somehow entered the nostrils of those gun wielding street dwellers like toxic fumes that consumed those movie characters who soon after became decrepit out for blood and brains zombies. I lived in the hood but did not grow up in the hood, was from the hood but not of the hood, at least not until later in life…

Deuteronomy chapter 28, verse 29:

"And thou shalt grope at noonday, as the blind gropeth in darkness, and thou shalt not prosper in thy ways: and thou shalt be only oppressed and spoiled evermore, and no man shall save thee."

The Black and Brown Movement founded in the middle of 1989, was completely developed by the summer of 1990. It started as a rock group by the name of PEACE (People's Equality and Cultural Empowerment) it didn't last too long since we didn't have a complete band and we sucked as musicians and vocalists. The concept of the Movement came from the James Brown song, "Say it loud, I'm Black and I'm proud." The concept was born, say it loud, we are Black, and we are Brown. Carlos (Barriga) brought the idea to us one day after hearing the song and where we grew up all we saw and knew was Black and Brown. From the Brocks', who were and are Black and Brown, to the Jones' and the Barrigas. From

B.P.S. (Black P Stone) to the Easy Riders, from the oldies soul music that was played out of Latin low riders.

Deuteronomy chapter 28, verse 30:

"Thou shalt betroth a wife, and another man shall lie with her: thou shalt build a house, and thou shalt not dwell therein: thou shalt plant a vineyard and shall not gather the grapes thereof."

It first started with us as youngsters on a musical endeavor. It was not until we realized that we were indulging in the same types of behavior and activities that we were supposed to be fighting against, that we decided this was also a social movement.

Earlier that year in April, Marques (other Founding Father of the Movement after Carlos bowed out), had an out of body/near death experience. The exact date was April 20, 1990, and Marques calls this his second birthday. When asked about this incident, to this day Marques gets chocked up and emotional as he puts it, "I got robbed!" He went on to elaborate that "at the same time I got blessed, but I got robbed of dreams. It made me stronger and everything, but when I look at it in hindsight, it kind of makes me upset to think of the ambitions I couldn't fulfill. On the flip side of that, I am blessed to be alive and have been able to be a father to my four beautiful daughters. I just want to grow as a person and continue to spread positive words to that community I am no longer a part of. 28th Street helped me to grow into the spiritual leader God created me to be, the Deuce Eight will always be my block and just made me into the warrior I am today, but Jesus is the reason I am here. I could have come out blastin', but he told me to walk with him and my heavenly father."

Deuteronomy chapter 28, verse 31:

"Thine Ox shall be slain before thine eyes, and thou shall not eat thereof: thine ass shall be violently taken away from before thy face, and shall not be restored to thee: thy sheep shall be given unto thine enemies, and thou shalt have none to rescue them."

I remember that night like it was yesterday as I was across the street at the Barriga's house, in the back. I heard the shots and remembered telling Carlos Barriga and his brother Luis, "Somebody just got blasted on (shot up)!" It is unfortunate that we had become so calloused to the sounds of gun shots, like living in a war-torn country like Vietnam. Not too long after hearing the shots, Carlos and Luis' sister Jackie came to the back and told us that it was Marques who was shot. Their eldest brother Chavo (Chavio) emerged from the Barriga house with his 9mm handgun as we stayed down in their yard surveying the block. It was Chavo who went across the street to find out that the culprits were already gone. The lasting and most disturbing image of that night was of Marques being lifted into the ambulance. As always, "Mr. Positive" left us with thumbs up and a, "I'm alright."

Deuteronomy chapter 28, verse 32:

"Thy sons and thy daughters shall be given unto another people, and thine eyes shall look, and fail with longing for them all the day long: and there shall be no might in thine hand."

We later found out that it was a case of mistaken identity as they were looking for one of Marques' friends (with friends like that, who needs enemies?) who had gone to the store for some beers. Marques had a gun in his apartment that night and as he later described, when the doorbell rang, he thought it was his friend coming back from the store. He opened the door immediately but did not see anyone until he looked in the bushes to the side of his apartment and instead of going back into the apartment or reaching for the gun that was near the front door, he ran on a walkway on the side of the apartment. His girlfriend at the time was in the house and this was another reason he said he did not run back in the house. The first shot we heard across the street, dropped Marques as it hit one of his knees. The other shots we heard came when Marques screamed for his mother in the apartment in front of his, while the gunman stood over him. One shot after another hit Marques everywhere but the vital parts of his body. There were thirteen bullets in all after the assassin had fled through the back alley.

Deuteronomy chapter 28, verse 33:

"The fruit of thy land, and all thy labours, shall a nation which thou knowest not eat up; and thou shalt be only oppressed and crushed away."

These curses from God went on from verses 15 – 68, getting worse with each curse. Before I knew God personally, there were times when bad things happened, and I was never there when they did. There was a time when Marques and Mixer were on the block and rivals from a surrounding hood drove through and acted like they were from our block, and when Marques and Mixer stopped to look, they shot at them. Through the grace of God, they were not hit, and I was not around. There was another time when other rivals from another hood drove through, and it was broad day light. Marques held off two gunmen with a Mac 11 (an automatic weapon) and again I was not around. I know now that everything happens for a reason and that God was with me, even when I had not accepted him in my heart and in my life and had not known him personally. As I mentioned earlier, I was born Catholic, until I turned sixteen and began to question the religion and why certain things were done and how they were done. I couldn't get a satisfactory answers and left religion alone until I turned 18 and studied religion in college (more on that later). God was with me the whole time and I didn't even know it.

I left for college at the end of the summer of 1990. I went to Humboldt State University from 1990 to 1992 and in those two years I represented the Black and Brown Movement. I began to develop and integrate the ideals of the Movement. Humboldt State had a population of about seven thousand students and a predominately Caucasian populous. I became a part of their history as a liaison officer between B.S.U. (Black Student Union) and M.E.Ch.A (Movimiento Estudiantil Chicanismo de Aztlan) the Latin equivalent. This is where the ideas and words became action. While I was in Northern California, the other "Founding Fathers" and "Young Profits" were in Southern California. While I was attending MEChA meetings, until becoming a member, they were surviving the hood and trying not to become gang members. I was attending BSU (Black Student Union) meetings while they were meeting for daily marijuana smoke sessions to maintain sanity. I eventually took office in MEChA, at first, I was the vice president and then president. As president I made it mandatory that MEChA members attend Black Student

Union meetings. Their members started to attend MEChA meetings, and we started attending each other's events and supporting each other's issues. This was Black and Brown on a grassroots level. Back at home there was no grass and there were no roots in the "Concrete jungle."

When I first touched down in Humboldt, I immediately noticed its beautiful backdrop, with the plush green forest just behind the campus. The campus and surrounding areas were hilly, and the beach and Pacific Ocean were just about 15-20 minutes to the west.

So, I'm showing up in a Lakers letterman jacket and a leather Raiders cap, not knowing the culture shock I was about to experience. I was assigned to a co-ed dorm on the top floor and my room was the last one at the end of the hall. As I am making my way to my room, I'm seeing the other students in the hall and in their rooms and hearing the music and the talk and laughter. The building is all a buzz while everyone is showing up and getting acclimated and settled in. Still on my way to my room with my bags in hand, I am pulled into one room, where they are drinking and smoking bud (weed). I was offered and accepted the provisions and greetings. I left that room and was pulled into another and another before I finally made it to my room at the end of the hall. The people I met looked, dressed, and listened to different music than me. My room had two rooms with a common living room. The rooms were small with bunkbeds, so four people assigned to the room. The first thing I see as I walk in the room is my roommates with a six-foot bong with a bean bag behind them. I asked what the bean bag was for, and they told me to hit the bong to find out. With a six-foot bong, someone must load and light the bowl while the other person starts to pull on the bong to fill it with six feet of smoke. This may take a couple of bowls to fill the bong. It is now full of smoke, and I was told to blow out as much air from my lungs as I can, then pull in as much smoke as I can from the bong. I did what I was told, and the mystery of the bean bag was revealed as I almost passed out and fell into the bean bag.

My roommate played saxophone and played in Humboldt's Jazz band and was in a local band, they had a lead guitar and drums and bass and my boy on sax. One day I went to a rehearsal with him at one of the band member's garages off campus. The band did not have a vocalist, and I had just began writing rhymes, so as I heard them playing a cover of the "War" song "Low Rider," I wrote some lyrics to the song that related to the local area's current times and culture. They liked what I wrote and the next thing you know we were performing at local house/keg parties. I wrote to a couple of other songs they were covering and a couple of originals as well. It was fun, and I gained vital experience performing with a live band verses flowing/rhyming to tracks. (Tracks can be considered electronic music.)

The interaction and feedback you get from a live musical performance is unmatched.

Musicians feed off each other and vocalists and musicians do the same. Audiences feed off musicians and vocalists. Music is more than an art/audio form, it is an experience. Music has always been a huge part and holds a majority percentage in all our lives, for all our lives since it describes who and where we are in our lives. The expression and emotion it can emulate from the human psyche is as necessary as memory. Imagination is the engine that drives the vehicle of dreams. I will never forget the first check I received for a performance; it came from the university and was for $2,500.00 for a twenty-minute set on our campus quad area. There is no better situation in this world than to be able to do what you love to do and get paid for it. There were smaller events such as panel discussions, meetings, caucuses, and poetry readings that kept me in the loop and close to the temperature of what was going on at those times. There was so much I wanted to know and learn and knew that I also had so much to offer as well but knew that there was such a long way to go to reach my destination.

"Destination to me is a goal, a height to be reached. Where I come from, tells me where I am going. God has given the vision and without works, faith is dead. Destination is achievement/effort = results. It is written. My destination has been predetermined.

With "cause and effect," I know that I can affect the cause. As I sit right here, right now! This is my destination! I am on route to a location TBA (to be announced) I keep good and evil at bay, as I know where the balance lies. Look into their eyes to identify whether they lie. They came from the skies in disguise. What was their destination? I'm not sure, but I am at mine, the end of this page." (A short "Spoken Word" piece from 1991)

*C*HAPTER 10

(1991) *Busta Rhymes appeared on A Tribe Called Quest's classic "Scenario", his style and voice were so outrageous and wild, making a new eccentric delivery in lyricism. KDAY was sold, and its All-Rap format ended. DJ David (Germany) won the DMC World DJ Championship two years in a row ('90 and '91). N.W. A's follow-up record, 1991's "Niggaz4Life," sold 954,000 copies in its first weeks of release and became the first hardcore rap album to hit No. 1 on the charts, despite being banned by some record stores and labeled by English authorities as obscene. Cypress Hill released its self-titled debut 'Cypress Hill'. The members B-Real, DJ Muggs and Sen Dog became supporters of hemp legalization and official musical spokesmen for the National Organization to Reform Marijuana Laws. Alternative rap ascended in popularity with groups such as De La Soul, A Tribe Called Quest, Digable Planets, Gang Starr, the Pharcyde and Arrested Development. Starring Ice Cube, it portrayed the lives of young Black men in South Central L.A., (Boyz N the Hood hit movie theaters nationwide.*

I was on a break from Humboldt and recollect being with my boyz, all greatly anticipating the premiere of "Boyz N the

Hood." We went to Universal City they now call "City Walk," to see the movie. I think it was Marques, Jesus, Carlos, Luis and me, the last three being Barriga brothers. I believe it was opening night, and a limo pulled up and the director of the movie, John Singleton steps out. Moments later a couple of gun shots rang out and I remember seeing this dude wearing white Levi jeans where one of pant legs was now red from blood since he had been shot in his leg. Everybody scattered frantically, and we made it back to the hood since the movie was cancelled. We would eventually go to and get to see this epic film, which is still an inspiration to me today.

I will never forget the IMC (International Multi-Cultural) poetry reading that I was blessed to be able to organize. I started out attending small poetry readings with about fifteen to twenty people, before I started reading other people's work and eventually my own. There were three highlights/ main events that I will never forget while at Humboldt State University. The first was the IMC poetry reading where two hundred and fifty people graced us with their presence. I had Aztec and African dancers, Chinese drummers, and an international multicultural potluck/poetry reading. The culture and art and expression represented there that day, was a spectacle to behold. I had been to a Native American Pow Wow (gathering/celebration and sharing of culture, from music to food to art to clothing and dance) in that region and at that time I did not know that I had Cherokee in my blood, and it was not until the brothers that I never knew I had, found me, that I found out. But this was beyond my wildest imagination and at the poetry reading, I read some of my work.

(My poem for International Multi-Cultural poetry reading)

"First it was the Indian, the native American, the indigenous peoples of this land who first fell victim to the colonization. First it was God's land and now it's the U.S. nation. He bumped into this land in 1492 Mr. Chris Colombo and his shipwrecked crew. Now he is a hero on certain date, because he discovered America in a most peculiar way. He discovered a land that was already there, my peoples had been there for many years. The European went to Africa and stole my brother, and then they went to Mexico and fucked another! This how and where it all began, the killing of the native man the stealing of the native land, the raping of our wives and daughters… They sailed across the ocean waters; before they came it was a spiritual society and now, we live in a material society."

There was some of the best and most diversified poetry that I have ever heard and some of the best I had ever written.

(Verse from The Black and Brown Movement song "It's supposed to be")

"Time has come for our peoples to rise up, wake up and open your eyes up…

Look, the bombs bursting in air…gave proof through the night that the war was still there…

Oh say can you see by the dawn's early dark, does that star strangled banner still wave? Time has come everybody, this land was not free, it was built on the backs of the slaves…

End up in a grave, government is manmade, political analytical hand grenade…

Who governs the government, the governors of irrelevance?

Their playing on our intelligence, we have got rhymes while they've got excuses…

Don't refuse this, just get used to this.

The only excuse for you is your self-inflicted mental abuses…

It is supposed to be the home of the brave and the land of the free…

But we're still modern-day slaves.

We're just not living in huts and caves, but if you misbehave, you might end up in a Grave."

Humboldt State University is a California state university (which was cheaper than a U.C. University of California school i.e., UCLA or UC Berkley) and was the farthest I could go from home and still be in the state. So, it was rough being that far away from what was going on back home and having to deal with these people who had no idea. I was given the opportunity to perform in the town square; this was outside of the campus and was in the community. It was a small community a small town, but it was still an opportunity to express my thoughts, opinions, and feelings. Although it was a small community, there was a huge turnout. It was as if folks from other local towns and neighborhoods had converged onto our college town square. I remember it was cool that morning, slightly overcast as it had been most of the time I was there, but I also remember the clouds parting and the sun rearing its beautiful yellow and orange and red head. I remember looking out over the stage with the town hall as its backdrop and seeing all these people and flashing back to a scene in my mind and seeing so many more people and seeing Jimi Hendrix and Carlos Santana on stage doing their respective things as it were. This was a microcosm of that scene, a mini "Woodstock" if you will. It was an awareness/consciousness concert that featured local bands and acts that they felt had relative material. I performed with my boy (vocalist) Johnny pathfinder and a drummer and an upright bass player.

(This was a verse from the song performed that day)

"We keep struggling and we keep pushing without pause. I'm a believer of this. Movement and ready to die for the cause. Like M.L.K. (Martin Luther King Jr.) Malcolm X, Julio Cesar Chavez and J.F.K. (John F Kennedy) Who is next? Who will look into the faces of every race to let them know there is none superior to we, I.M.C. (International Multi-cultural)? We're prejudge by the color of our skins, not where we are going or where we've been. We're not numbers or statistics. We've got our own traits and characteristics. When you think about it, think holistically, clear your mind, soul and vision and think realistically. In the past we've been quiet, when peace they don't buy it, here comes the riot. They kicked us down, we kept our heads up We broke from the bread and drank from the cup. One day we'll be at the table with Jesus, but don't worry because he sees us. Whether you believe in my God or whether you believe in Jah. Whether you believe in my God or whether you believe in Allah. Whoever you're God may be, give praise to him or her and he or she will see. To some this may come as a surprise, we're all brothers and sisters in God's eyes."

The third and final event of my Humboldt experience was opening for "Cypress Hill." (a Hip-Hop group based out of Los Angeles and was hot at that time) It was toward the end of my second year, and I was able to get those guys to start their tour at Humboldt State University. Through the pull I had generated over the two years I had spent at H.S.U. I was able to raise a budget of about $10,000.00 and after paying them $5,000.00 dollars for a twenty-minute set and covering their travel expenses and room and board; I was still able to pay myself $1,500.00 for a ten-minute opening set. I realized early that besides getting a hold of their management, convincing them to perform in Humboldt, was not that great of a task. Humboldt County has always been known and infamous for their cultivation of marijuana and just like Humboldt, Cypress Hill was known for marijuana as well.

(Verse from The Black and Brown Movement song "Back to the Stoned Ages")

"Opened the book and turned the pages, we're taking you back to the stoned ages. This is where we've had our share of suffering, Dr. Tom Slick is trying to slide us Bufferin and Advil and Tylenol, all we really need is THC (tetrahydrocannabinol)

Combined with delta nine, it grows on a stem and not a vine. I find the mystical crystals are so divine to thine mind. The dialectic gets hectic, the sound is phonetic. It's celestial, extraterrestrial. Someday you'll find that dealing with the doctor is like dealing with proctor, you're gambling on. Like Led Zeppelin, I keep a "Ramblin' on." We find elevation when the Movement makes improvements in our relations between the nations. Unification brings about an overwhelming sensation. The hemp conscience is ready for invasion check the equation as we commence to blazing… ain't much phasing me, more than God's glory as we still raising our children by wielding a message in not yielding the right of way, until we see a brighter day. You have to pay to play"

The on-campus auditorium held about seven thousand and I remember seeing a comedy show with my girlfriend at the time, the comedian was Sandra Bernhard, she was hilarious! So, I was finishing my ten-minute opening set, and the crowd started to go crazy. I thought maybe because I was the local act, they were appreciating me, but of course I was mistaken. I turned around and saw that Cypress had already set up behind me and their lead MC "B Real" stepped onto the stage wearing a Humboldt baseball jersey and cap with his afro sticking out of it. He handed me the fattest dubbie (marijuana joint) I had ever seen in my life, even "Cheech & Chong" had nothing on this one. He handed it to me, and I handed him the microphone as the music dropped and they began their set.

When I was backstage with Cypress Hill, we were "freestylin" (a form of a hip hop expression where the rhymes said are thought of as they are being said) and Cypress asked me to go on tour with them after I had battled (freestylin against another MC) "Everlast." (Much love and respect to him) They gave me a day to think about it, since they were leaving the next day. After thinking long and hard about it, I decided to let them know that I needed to figure out what I was going to do with school and my career and that I would see them when I got there. Some people think that I should regret that decision, but I do not. My life may have been different, and that is just it. I refuse to live with regrets, and I do not regret how my life turned out. They did tell me that if I was not going to go with them, that I should make my way back down to L.A., where the action was/is for the music industry. So, it was time for another road trip.

(Verse from The Black and Brown Movement song "Traveling, taking trips")

"You can call me the traveling man, me and my family roll like a band of gypsies. You can't get with these, sometimes we caravan like a clan of hippies. In our stash, is our herbs and our hash and when you take trips, you gots to have cash. If you want to smash, you gots to have gas and if you want to see the squeegee has got to hit the glass. When trippin the pad becomes my screen and pen becomes my camera. Why does it seem that you've never seen this much stamina? Pops was a rolling stone, until he fell victim to the glass bone. When he began to roam, the streets became his home, and this is the picture that will never leave my dome. So, I take it with me on my own journey. I'll catch you in traffic if you can catch my geographic position, on a spiritual mission when we came to a fork in the road. We saw a wise "Veterano" (veteran) who told us "this Movement will be a very heavy load, for one to carry on their shoulders." He pulled out a flask and told us to take a sip as we got back to our travels and on our trip"

Before I left Humboldt there was a trip, however it didn't involve the road as I was flying out to Chicago in the summer of 1991. My second year at Humboldt, early in the year, I met Cynthia at a M.E.ChA meeting. She was into Gothic music and dress, which was different from what I had dated before that, but I was attracted to her dark and big eyes, short and sexy haircut, and her olive skin. We fell in love at our young age, and she wanted me to be at her sister's wedding with her, that summer. She bought me a suit when I touched down, I was out there for a couple of weeks. I was taken to downtown Chicago for the tour, between the museums and the Sears tower, I was treated like the typical tourist. After the wedding, that same week, she surprised me by taking me to "La La Palooza," a summer concert tour that happened to be in Chicago that weekend. We went and had the time of our lives. The headliners were "Red Hot Chili Peppers," "Ice Cube," "Stone Temple Pilots," "Pearl Jam," the lineup was sick. (Very good) We started out at the side stage where we saw the "Boo Ya Tribe" and none other than Cypress Hill. "B Real" (Cypress Hill's lead MC) was wearing a Humboldt baseball cap; I made my way to the stage after their performance and showed "B" my Black and Brown Movement logo tattoo. He remembered me and took my girl and I backstage with them; we got a chance to meet Ice Cube and the Chili Peppers. Come to find out, the newest lead guitarist of the Chili Peppers (at that time) was a friend from high school. That was a day I knew I would not forget. It was a grey and gloomy day, weather wise, it rained, and the lawn seating became a mudslide area. Mud was slung like food in a school cafeteria food fight. At some point, the situation got out of hand, and someone was trampled on in a stampede of concert goers who now resembled a heard of buffaloes being hunted by my ancestors. Ambulance and on-site paramedics rushed to the scene and aid of the injured patron, since as they say the show must go on and it did and was one of the best shows I've seen to date.

When I was in Humboldt, towards the end, everybody was telling me I had to leave. Everyone I associated with in the music to my MECHA and BSU affiliates. They all said to me that I needed to take what I had done in microcosm to the big stage and macrocosm of the metropolis of Los Angeles. As most people know, Los Angeles and Hollywood are the Mecca of entertainment. I followed their advice and took myself back to where I came from.

One of the main reasons I left Humboldt to come home was the fact that my mom was pregnant with her fifth and final child, my baby sister Amanda. I had not missed a previous birth of one of my siblings and although I left for home, I didn't make it back in time as my sister was born before I got there. This started a whole new chapter.

When I got back, I was slapped back into reality. It is funny how our imaginations create images in our minds based on certain things we are told whether it's the way they are presented or whether it is how we perceived them. My partner at the time and co-founder of the Black and Brown Movement, Carlos Barriga, was telling me the whole time that I was in Humboldt that he was down here (LA) with "Ice T" (one of the West Coast's first "Gangsta" rappers) at his house and in the studio with one of his producers. When I got home, I later found out that he was chilling with a "kat" (guy) we went to school with and his big brother, who was working with Ice T's "Rhyme Syndicate." They were a production team and crew of artists that were under Ice T. "Everlast," at some point was known to be a part of Rhyme Syndicate. (The same Everlast that I battled backstage with Cypress Hill) I guess he did go to Ice T's house, through the invite of our boy Canon and his brother. We worked with him for a while, Canon was a DJ and he added some "cuts and scratches" to the songs. We basically did one song after which… Canon was killed by an eighty-year-old man, who hit him with his car while Canon was hitching another car. He was a tow truck driver at the time. After Canon died, it affected his brother to the point that he stopped doing anything related to music. RIP Canon.

(A line from a Black and Brown Movement song "Ghetto Winds")

"Sippin' Hennessy as we sit and reminisce and wish we didn't have to live like this."

That incident became the first of many ventures with producers who usually were already working with other artists and the first experience of death within the Movement and in relation to the music. Unfortunately, it was not the last. When we would first hook up with a potential music producer, it seemed like even if they saw the potential of our talent and concept of our monumental musical movement, (as I like to call it) they would not completely buy into it. I do not know if it was a matter of pride or fear. Were they too proud to think that we could come in and be better than everything else they had been working with? Did they fear that what they had done to that point would not be as successful as us? Or was it a combination of both? They say that people are afraid of success. I believe it is the fear of failing that keeps them from taking the necessary risks needed to succeed. I lost count of the numerous managers, producers, DJs, MCs and promoters that came and went. Each of them with their own set of pipe dreams (when people tell you that they can do things for you when either they really can't or don't intend to in the first place).

(Verse from a Black and Brown Movement song "Pipe Dreams")

"People out there are selling pipe dreams, you got to move on and do your own thing. People out there are selling pipe dreams, you've got to move on, and you got to move on.

I was sold a pipe dream for a G ($1,000.00) a month to ride the "G Hound" (Greyhound Bus) and put on a front. I trimmed my beard and my mustache, so I could pass as the typical white boy college kid. Pulled off the bid and got rid of the package. I knew that I could manage in doing damage, so yo, let's handle this. Left the station from downtown Los Angeles heading west, on my way to do some business. What is this? "I'm a police officer; I need to ask you a few questions." "Where's your ticket? What's your name?

Can I see some identification?" I wanted to say I'm THC ("Time has Come" "The Hard Core" "The hemp Conscious" just a few acronyms for my stage name) from the Black and Brown nation, but then I knew I'd be facing immediate termination. "It's on my bag on the bus. Do you want me to go get it?" He said, "no don't fuss." At that point I knew my color had just saved me from the rusty bars, the cuts, and the scars and now I'm having visions of stars and Mars. I had to throw down the pipe and stop dreaming and start screaming... People out there are selling pipe dreams, you gots to move on, you got to move on."

$\mathscr{C}$HAPTER 11

(1992) *Protests and riots ensued in Los Angeles after the police officers who beat Rodney King were acquitted. Ice-T and Public Enemy's Chuck D were asked to comment to the media as hip-hop artists who became spokespeople for African American communities. Protests from law enforcement forced Time Warner to pull Ice-T's new group Body Count's song "Cop Killa" from its album. Dr. Dre's "The Chronic," West Coast gangsta rap starts to rule hip-hop with the solo album, featuring the wildly popular single "Nuthin' But a 'G' Thang." Dr. Dre and Suge Knight formed Death Row Records, with a recording featuring the up-and-coming rapper Snoop Doggy Dogg.*

The second most memorable event of the spring of 1992 was the brutal police beating of Rodney King. I was just getting news of the L.A. riots. The cops who beat Rodney King got off?!?! I hit the phone and spoke with my peoples who told me of stories about fires and smoke and looting and destruction and their confrontations/altercations with the police. I could hear gunshots in the background. I remember talking to a couple of my boys who had been to the local "swap meet" and other local businesses, they told me about the shoes, clothes, and jewelry that they "came up on" (came up = getting for free) from looting. In the meantime, there were panel discussions and so much buzz on campus, it was such a contrast to the stories I had heard from my sources. I sat with these intellectuals while they were analyzing the situation, knowing that my family was down in LA going through it. It was frustrating to think that as the oldest son and sometimes man/head of our household, I was so far away and felt paralyzed by not being able to help. If anything, I would have had the ability to help my family and friends deal with and get through the situation. I heard that Ricky (Ricks' son) was hit with an egg while walking down the street. He looked white with his green eyes, more than he did Mexican or Native American. I worried for my mother and baby sister Amanda who were in that same situation. Rick himself looked only/solely white with his long dirty blonde hair but was a grown man with the ability to look after himself, which I prayed he did for my mother, since I knew he would for his precious Amanda. (She was his only child he had with my mother, and he sheltered her and treated her like a princess and my siblings like pheasants.)

Being away during that epic time in LA history was somewhat hard for me, that was my home, where I grew up. Knowing that what my peoples were going through and I was not there with them, had me feeling a little guilty. So, let me transition back to us dealing with the music industry and people in general who we felt never wanted to see us succeed. In another time and space.

It was not just the people in the industry who were selling pipe dreams. It was people in the streets, it was family and supposed friends. It was people in business and people in non-profit. As I said, this Movement was based in music, but evolved and developed into something that reflected the lives we lived and chose to live. The paths we chose and sometimes were forced to travel. When I think about the road I rumbled down, I know my direction was backwards. Most success stories that I have heard, were about people who had some troubles in their childhood or teenage years and were able to turn it around later in their lives. In my case, being forced to be so responsible so young, helped me to be successful at an early age. I had good grades in school, played sports, was involved in extracurricular activities, and was blessed to be gone (usually to camp) most summers. Yosemite was two of those summers, in a row. Besides a couple of incidents when I was a teenager, I was a pretty good kid and I believe and hope that mom would agree.

Although, there was that one Christ-mas (X-mas) that we spent at my aunt/Godmother Teresa's house, when I was sixteen. My cousin Marcus woke up early that X-mas morning and woke me up, and said, "let's roll" and we did. Our first stop was one of his friend's spots where we picked up a half ounce of low-grade marijuana and stole a fifth of Jack Daniels. Need I say more? Other than the fact that we didn't stumble back to his garage/room at my aunt's house until later that evening, and by the time anybody had realized that we had made it back, it was one of my older cousins and uncles who came in and turned on the light to find my cousin Marcus sprawled and passed out on his bed and me on his couch. They made us get up and made a big commotion as they were pushing us around and cursing us out for making our mothers and Grannymom (our nickname for our grandmother) worry. Rick (mom's husband) even tried to come in and be part of the act. My cousins and uncles were not allowing that. They told him to go back in the house as they had it covered. I still consider that day as good times had, with a not-so-great ending.

I was the only one in my family to go to college straight out of high school. I always felt the pressure of that fact and knowing that I was expected to succeed. I was looked at differently by my family members as compared to some who did not finish school or who may have gotten into drugs or gangs or just did not see a future for themselves outside of that.

I remember they threw me a huge party to send me off after my high school graduation. The party was also for my uncle Johnny who graduated from UCLA that year, he was thirty at the time. My grandfather was there, and I remember that because he was not part of my life. I got the 411 (info) from my family that grandpa was on a short leash with his wife of so many years, who was after my Grannymom of course. I later got the other side of the story that Grannymom had upset his wife and that was why she didn't want to deal with her which included her children and grandchildren. Although, I can say that he did deal with some of his children, and he did give me some money to send me off. I still to this day am disappointed that I did not have a relationship with him. The party was one of our usual family parties. There was plenty of food and drinks flowing, music blasting and everyone had fun. Our neighbors agreed to park on the street and clear out our underground parking garage. We set up tables and decorations and family I hadn't seen in a long time came down from the Bay Area (San Francisco) It was the best sendoff I could have asked for.

When I came back from Humboldt though, things got rough with Rick at mom's house. I went to stay with my Tia Teresa and my primos in La Puente California. She let me stay in a small trailer that was in her back yard at the time. I was there for about 6 months and there were some definite memories that were created there. My auntie and cousins were and always have been major party people. My cousin Adrian who is a couple of years older than me, always knew where the good parties where at. I would roll with him when I could and remember having to present my case to the "Techno," "Trance/Dance" (genres of music) DJ's. All they did was play and mix music, maybe an occasional shout out or an introduction of themselves would get them on the "mic," otherwise there were no MC's (Master of Ceremonies / Mic Controller) I had to learn how to flow (rap) to Techno and Trance music since that's all they played.

So, we went to house and warehouse techno rave parties, I approached every DJ to rock the Mic. After a while, the DJs would recognize me and my cousin and he was part of what they called back then, a "party crew." This was a group of party goers who would plan and promote their own parties or would go to other parties and represent their crew. It got to a point where we started to implement hip-hop into our own parties and began MC battles. The most infamous battle was between us and "Latin Alliance." (a Hip-Hop group associated with Kid Frost, another Legendary Latin LA Hip-Hop artist) This was a battle that we won. It was my little brother Silas, this kat named Lucky, our DJ (Samoan) and myself. I met the DJ and this guy Lucky at my aunt's house. As I mentioned before, my family loved to party and there was always something going on at their house. This is how I met them as they knew my cousin and would come by to practice DJing and MCing.

We ended up putting the party and MC battle together with Latin Alliance and started practicing freestyle battling at my aunt's house when DJ Samoan brought his turntables over. Shortly after the party and MC battle of the year, I went home for a visit to LA and

I will never forget the time Lucky took me with him to meet a female friend of his in-Silver Lake. This friend eventually became my first "baby's momma." Her name is Nina, and she already had two boys when I met her. She is Puerto Rican, her father molested her, her mother is a lesbian, her oldest brother is homosexual, and her younger brother was a drug addict and in and out of prison. I say all that just to give a little background on what I learned about how she grew up, about her life, and about what she had gone through before I met her. There were just quite a few different dynamics within her family setting that were contributing factors to her upbringing. I later found out that the father of her boys was abusive. I wish this portion of the story that introduces my first-born child were much longer and a lot more positive, but unfortunately it is not. I was young and had enough of my own background that attracted me to her.

When Nina first told me she was pregnant, I told her that I would support any decision she would make and would live up to my responsibility. She told me two weeks after she found out, I did not hear from her again until 5 months into the pregnancy when she had just gotten back from a clinic finding out that it was too late to abort. I did not hear from her again until two weeks after my daughter Aurora Lestinia was born. I was able to see her for the first time and was able to see myself in her. I saw her off and on, more off than on, the first two years of her life. Aurora Lestinia Levine Fonseca is her name and unfortunately for me, I have not seen her since she was two, she is now headed into her twenties and is in the Air Force from what I heard.

I was able to track her mother down some years back and ironically, she lived only a couple miles away from me at the time. I remember taking my wife Nikki and my two boys, Juwan, and Josiah. Juwan was old enough to have an idea of what was going on and he had seen a picture of his sister when she was two and asked who she was. I told him and for a while he was sad about knowing that he had a sister somewhere out there and he couldn't see her. He cried sometimes out of the blue when he thought about her.

So, we go over to the address which had been only a couple of miles away from where I lived, and we pulled up when we found it. I walked up to an apartment with Juwan by my side and Nina came to the door. She looked as if she had seen a ghost. I was smiling on the inside. I introduced her to my son and told her that he wanted to meet his sister. She stepped out of the house and walked me to the front of the apartment complex as I peeked inside her apartment trying to at least catch a glimpse of my daughter. This is how I know she was there that evening. Nina started telling me about how I hadn't tried to see her in all the previous years and how she hasn't told her about me and how she didn't want her to know about me. We argued for a while and her man (husband?) came out and he took me to the side and told me that he didn't want to get involved and that he could relate with me, which was a relief to discover. Nina told him to go back in the house and call her mother (my daughter's grandmother) and I believe she was telling him to take my daughter to her.

She admitted to me that she had allowed her mother (my daughter's grandmother) to adopt my daughter when she was one years old. I saw my daughter up until she was two. Nina didn't list me on my daughter's birth certificate and her excuse was that she didn't want me to get harassed for child support when really, she didn't want me to have any rights as a father. Aurora was my first child and Nina knew the game while I didn't, and she played the game and she played me. I left peacefully, and my wife and I met with a family lawyer who advised us that I would need to get a paternity test to prove that I am the biological father and that would allow her to get the adoption revoked since by law, you must have both parents agree or sign off on an adoption.

Nina was constantly moving and disappearing, and I was not able to catch up to her again. It wasn't until years later that my wife was able to find her on Facebook and had a conversation with her. My wife was even able to speak with my daughter who was now becoming of legal age. Nina told her that she was diagnosed with cancer and thought she was going to die. Based on that and her guilt, she finally told my daughter about me. My daughter was of course upset, more than the fact that I existed, was the fact that the man that raised her was not her father. She did not want to speak to me according to my wife and was opened to possibly meeting her siblings. That hasn't happened, and this is years later. My wife lost contact with Nina. I pray for my daughter and Nina and have given it to God.

Not too long after I returned from college, I was called back for a performance that was lined up and we were asked to be the opening act. The headliners were "The Untouchables," a "Ska" band. "Ska" is a sub-genre of Reggae music and "The Untouchables" were an accomplished and seasoned band with a great amount of popularity within the fan base of the genre. So, some of my folks from Humboldt made the arrangements and paid our way up, including accommodations and paid us for the performance. Since I hadn't been gone for too long, most of my friends, school mates and roommates were still there. I guess I had built some sort of local fan base, which is why we got the call. So, Carlos was still hanging in as the other 'Founding Father" (of the Movement) at the time and Silas had started getting involved with the music and we also got DJ Samoan and Lucky to take the trip with us. I was able to co-ordinate my previous drummer, upright bass and my boy Johnny Pathfinder who was a talented vocalist I worked well with when I was there. The performance worked out well, was fun and it was extremely unforgettable meeting "The Untouchables." We partied with them after the show and again at an after party that my peoples from Humboldt had thrown for us. I remember Silas getting drunk and throwing up at the party; he was still young, but that never stopped him from trying to keep up and going hard. (That applied to anything he did, which obviously could be good or bad, depending on what it was) After a couple of days, we made our way back down to LA and attempted to build off that momentum.

Lucky came with me to my neighborhood. I took him to introduced him to my peoples. Marques was suspicious of him from the beginning and always had a good feel for people and could see clearly through any fake bullshit, he had a radar for it. Come to find out, Lucky was a Crip (LA gang) or associated with them and he tried to get us to come to a party in Altadena. Marques recognized the neighborhood he was trying to get us to come to as an Altadena Crip hood. It was a setup and of course we didn't go and never saw Lucky again after that.

*C*HAPTER 12

(1993) Staten Island's Wu Tang Clan released their hard-hitting debut, Enter the Wu-Tang: 36 Chambers, it reinvigorated the East Coast rap scene with the single "C.R.E.A.M.

Salt-N-Pepa's "Very Necessary" is the best-selling album of all time by a female artist or group.

Snoop Doggy Dogg's "DoggyStyle" became the first debut album to enter the Billboard charts at number one, while Snoop was being charged with second-degree murder. Sean "Puffy" Combs started Bad Boy Entertainment, a record label he ran out of his apartment)

When we were young, there were those family parties that were either held at our house or my Aunt Theresa's house. There was always plenty of alcohol at those parties; a good majority of my family are alcoholics, thanks to "GrannyMom" (my grandmother, whose story will be told later). When the adults were drunk and halfway passed out, we would creep by the dining table and scoop up the half and quarter full glasses of wine or whatever other liquor they were drinking. We started drinking at an early age like most of the rest of our family. I thank God every day that I am not able to drink like most of my family as my stomach won't allow it. I usually get sick before I get drunk and can't stand to deal with that as much as the pleasure of drinking or getting drunk. Unfortunately for Silas and the rest of my family, they didn't have the same problem as they succumbed to the disease of alcoholism.

It wasn't until I got back from Humboldt that I decided to go to the dark side. I'm not sure if it was the fact that I was tired of being good after all those years or if it was out of frustration about my home life. I came back after two years of college. Ultimately, I realized that the real reason I turned 180° was based in one word, "balance." One of the main mantras of mine is "balance is the key to life." I grew up in the hood and knew nothing about it. My circumstances contributed to my decisions and actions at that time. In retrospect, it made me the well-rounded person I became to this day. I'm not proud of a lot that I did from that point, but I had to learn the difference between right and wrong through experience.

Music always took a backseat to survival. I always said the same thing about school, if you don't have the right support system, you will not be successful in a higher institute of learning. That doesn't just mean one thing. There are multiple contributing factors to a good support system. The first is usually financial; if you are too worried about where your next meal is coming from or how you are going to pay rent and bills, you won't be able to concentrate and focus on academics. The second is usually drama; if you have issues at home, whether it's with a spouse or siblings or any other family members or roommates. When it's time to study and do homework, if you don't have a quiet place/space and you have someone in your face, you just can't get it done. The third and final factor that can detour you and keep you out of school, is self. When you don't believe that you can overcome the first two above factors and you don't have the confidence that you can compete, you begin to doubt yourself. Those excuses become crutches that you can't stand on, let alone walk without. For the first time in my life, those first two main factors drove me out of my house and into the streets of the neighborhood.

See I had just gotten back from Humboldt and a lot had happened in the two years I was gone. My mom at some point went to Las Vegas I believe and married Rick, they had been married for those two full years I was gone. I hadn't enrolled in school yet and didn't have a job when I got back. I immediately felt the tension in the home, now just a house that I grew up in.

At this point is when I started hanging out with my brother Marques, up the hill on the deuce eight block. When Marques and I first met, I was twelve, and he was fourteen, on 28th Street. There was street ball being played, either baseball (using a tennis ball) or it was football. I used to think I was Steve Largent from the Seattle Seahawks out there on the street playing football, catching passes, and running into cars sacrificing my young body. I had NO speed but could run a route and catch anything thrown my way. Either way, I can say that we did not like each other from the start. I thought he talked too much shit. (trash) The first thing he ever said to me or directed at me was as I was joining the game, "who's the white boy?" When interviewed, Marques said what he thought when he first met me, "Who's this funny white kid in the ghetto? You were different and always stuck out like a sore thumb, but you were cool after a while."

He always said that I was scared to hang out on the block, and he was right as I remember playing in the alley behind my apartments with my cousins. We found a dead body in a "bucket." (old beat-up car) What were we doing playing in an alley? I don't know, but I do remember thinking the man was sleeping in the car. I think our ball bounced near the car and my cousin went to get it when he noticed the smell. We found out later that the body had been there for more than a week. That image and more potently that stench, still linger in that alley to this day.

That alley was never good news. When my brother was ten and I was fifteen, my brother was hit and run over by a car in that alley. He was running to buy a bag of chips and jumped out in front of the car. If the lady had slammed on the breaks the same way she did the gas pedal, my brother would not be alive today. Instead of the weight of the car crushing him, the car rolled over him and spit him out of the back. I remember being scared to death not knowing how hurt my brother was. In all honesty, I remember thinking how angry my mom would be, cause I'm the oldest, and it was my responsibility and my fault. Instead of being killed, he ended up with a broken femur bone (thigh bone) in one of his legs. I remember running out to the alley and seeing him lying there, his leg was twisted like a pretzel and his thigh was three times its regular size. He was in such shock, that he didn't even cry or scream. He eventually ended up in a body cast for six months and we had to wipe his ass, but we still loved/love him.

After I got over my fear of being out on the block, it began from nickel bags of weed to dimes, to twenty sacks to half and whole ounces, to quarter to half pounds to whole pounds (weed, herbs, bud, stress, chronic / all street slang for marijuana) As Marques calls it, "The ghetto life environment, survival mode." I began spending more and more time up the hill. It began with spending the night until it turned into living with and keeping up with the Jones'.

Marques talked about how it made him laugh every time we talked about him getting me out on the block…" When this nigga came back from Humboldt, Moms abandoned him and moved to Seattle and we were kickin' it and I figured that if he was gonna be with me on the block while I was street hustling, he needed to know the ropes to be able to maintain and not get caught in the trap. We were down on the block chillin and just standing around and scoping the situation and observing thangs, you know what street hustlers do, and then suddenly, he would say, "hey man I got to go up the hill real fast and use the bathroom." But I already peeped my boy was nervous, and a lil scared, you know this was a whole new saga for him. He grew up in the hood, but he never hung out in the hood, which was on Montclair, where every thang went down!!!"

Again, I am not proud of contributing to the genocide of my people.

(A verse from Black and Brown Movement song "Not Proud of our Actions")

"Not proud of my actions, never confused by the factions of gang banging or hustling, making money or muscling, I've been on the block when Katz got shot, film containers full of rocks, pockets full of knots, starting with sums of crumbs to almost slanging tons. Been up yawning, crack of dawn, wee hours of the morning, mingled with coins and singles to nicks, dubs and Ben Franks, from 2's and fews to big bank, went from dry dummy to floods of blood money, spent it faster than could get it, it can catch you if you let it. Never like these mean streets, a means to an end, sometimes only way to eat, it was always stress and strife, wasn't bout that gang life, learned how to grab my pad and pen, so I didn't end up in the pen or body dead with soul in the wind. A life of sin, more lose than win, been more out than in, the house of the Lord, know his word is that double-edged sword, not gonna front or lie to ya, not gonna preach or cry to ya, but if you real in this revolution, I will die with ya. The life we once lived, not proud of it but it's how we survived in this bullshit from the deuce eight to the bull pit It's how we survived, contributing to genocide. The life we once lived, not proud of it, those corrupt streets, from the deuce eight to the bull put it's how we survived, contributing to genocide.

Another example of us God's curses?

(Marques' verse for "Not Proud of our Actions")

"At age 13 I was on my hustle, learned to use my mind, didn't have to use my muscle, at age 16 I got that sack of them rocks, started on the block, started to clock, not knowing the 1st thing about slangin' that cane, while the OG's was bangin' insane, out for a name and that street fame, I stayed in my lane and did my thang, with the cocaine Regan era of the '80s, carried a 6 shot 380, graduated to a Mac 11, street educated, what's the difference

between hell or heaven? If you scared, go to church, and pray with your reverend, I remember too many dead homies and family members, too many bullets flying and too many mothers crying, sitting back and asking God why?"

When I started selling drugs, (crack to be exact) I will never forget the first sack (package) that I sold. It was a crumb sack that was worth at least $100.00, and I got beat since I ended up selling it for $12.00. One of the neighborhood's "smoker vets" got me good on that one, but never again. After that incident, Marques had to tell me to make sure and give them some "love" (a little extra) to keep them coming back. I had been doing it for a while and remember another time when it was about three or four in the morning. I was standing under a tree with about ten to fifteen "smokers" around me while I "served" (sold) them and when I was done and it was over, they dispersed like roaches when the lights are turned on. For those who don't know what "crack" is, it is cocaine cooked with baking soda to create a rocked substance. It is also called "rock," but "crack" refers to when the pieces that are smoked out of a glass pipe are cracked off the bigger rock piece. When selling "crack," you usually become rather proficient at cracking or shaving the pieces of rock. When outside on the street and there was no access to a razor, you learned how to use your fingernails.

There was another time when I was out on the "block," it was early evening and I had been down there for a few hours, making money. I had my "work" (product/crack) in a camera film container. (35mm) The "crash" (a gang unit for L.A.P.D.) unit rolled up, there were about fifteen of us. There were BPS

(Black P Stone) and Easy Rider gang members and there were a few of us hustlers, selling crack or weed. "Crash" rolled up in three cars and at least six to eight detectives hopped out. They lined us up against the brick wall on the side of "Dave's" liquor store. I tossed the film container in some tall grass as I got tossed up against that brick wall; then I stood there and waited to get frisked, while I was shitting bricks the whole time and hoping they didn't find that container. They didn't find it and I came back to retrieve it later that night.

(Black and Brown Movement song, "Lucky Luciano")

"Gather around now, gather around. I'm about to give you a bird's eye view into the life of a kid, from a boy to a man, from the crib to the bed pan. Take this mental walk with me, kaleidoscope of catastrophe. This is a street story; he thought glory...nah, more like blaspheme...He woke up early in the morning to start his routine. He had to run some errands for Moms and had to make sure the vegetables were clean. He hit the NY streets known as "Little Italy." He passed an alley on the way to the vegetable stand; this is where he saw the $2k (G) Armani suit man with a bat in his hand. He was standing next to a trash can, and he knew the money would exchange hands. He didn't see it, but at his young age he knew the plan. His eyes began to scan the block, looking for "Lucky" with the truck that's stocked. He waited patiently for his box, to deliver to the smoke shop for a small knot. Up to this point, he hadn't got caught. But then...he didn't listen to the sign that said stop! He ran up in the spot, not knowing it was hot! Five minutes later, it got lit up by the cops. Cut to the scene of the smoke shop, Lucky walked up and looked at a cop and gave him an eye. The kid's handcuffs were unlocked. The kid was shocked! At that

moment he just knew he couldn't be stopped! He figured out that the cops had been bought. Cut to the next scene, the kid no longer in his teens, but in his mid-20s. He was still working for Lucky plenty. Mr. Luciano took him under his wing; he knew he would never sing. Since he was a kid, he would always bring hustle to the table. He knew he was able, number one thorough bred out his stable. He knew he could kill more than a roach, so he became his batting coach. His approach was to make him the most feared hit man in the city, like "Frank Nitty." You would be lucky if you ever got the Luciano. Don't front, you know you used to love "Lucy" and "Ricky Ricardo." Mi nombre is De Franco, soy Xicano, Mexicano and Italiano. I'm storytelling to this beat homemade by "Benny Blanco." When he was the kid, he wanted to live "Lone Ranger." But instead, he was a Tonto always living in danger. He wanted to ride "Silver," but got bucked by a bronco and now he's riding "Tonka" trucks. He ain't got shit to lose, so he really doesn't give a Fuck! He feels like he's stuck in a scene from "Bugsy Malone," these thoughts, nightmares and dreams won't leave him alone. All he sees is pies of cream, he woke up and saw chrome pointed between his eyes...headed straight for his dome and now it's on."

I can not forget the day when my little brother Josiah came up the hill on the deuce-eight block, he was crying, and he told us that my mom's husband Rick had hit him with an extension cord. It was Marques, "Mixer" (Luis Barriga, brother of Carlos Barriga) and I. Before I continue, I must prelude this by saying that Rick had his issues. See Rick is white, Native American, and Mexican. I believe he grew up poor in a predominantly Mexican neighborhood and joined the local Mexican gang. I think his biggest issue was identity crisis, being of a similar racial makeup, I also had some of the same issues. When I was younger, there was always some sort of racial tension in our family which, in my opinion was mostly of outside, societal influences. When Rick came to live with us, at some point he ventured out in the hood and didn't get the results I think he was looking for. He was reminded that this was not his hood, and he was hustled out of some money, when he tried to buy some weed. I believe this created some resentment towards my brothers who are/were half Black. He tried getting me riled up a few times, through talking shit (trash) or throwing something at me, but I never bit.

So, when my brother Josiah came up the hill that day crying, I knew Rick had gone too far. I know he tried disciplining my brothers through punishment or his infamous school like standards. I know there was a time when my little brother decided to pull a broom on him, to let him know he wasn't scared. That day we went down the hill and around the corner to 4230 West Adams Boulevard, Apartment #102. When we got there, as soon as I walked in the door, Rick was standing there waiting for me. The first thing he said was, "I know you have a gun." I calmly let him know that I didn't need a gun. Little did he know, Marques did have a chrome, six shot 380. Rick said we should go down to the carport to fight, I told him no. He said we should go to the patio, I again told him no and advised him that I wanted everyone in the hood to see me whip that ass. I told him that I would be outside waiting for him. 5 minutes later he came outside, looked at all three of us and walked over to his truck, climbed in, and drove off. I did not see him again until I helped move my mom up to Washington State. I guess he went and got an apartment for a couple of months until he made his way to Seattle. So of course, a couple of months later my mom followed him up there. My little brother Silas did not want to go up there and begged my mom to let him stay with me. She decided to let him stay with me and she took my little brother Josiah and my sisters Amber and Amanda. It was ironic that just a few months before that, Marques, Mixer, and I were watching as Rick hopped into his truck and rolled out. (Drove off) And now us same three as well as my brother's Silas and Josiah, drove a huge "Ryder" truck, dragging (towing) my mom's bucket behind. We made plans that we would stop in Humboldt on the way to Seattle Washington. So, it's me, Marques, Mixer, and my two little brothers Silas and Josiah. It was basically Marques and I switching shifts and driving. I think it was Mixer who came up on some acid. (LSD) we "dropped" (took it) just before we left, on our way to Humboldt (a twelve-hour trip) both on the road and in our minds and bodies.

Marques myself and mixer dropped for sure, I couldn't remember if Silas did or not.

I know Josiah didn't. It was a hell of a trip, literally, after twelve hours we finally made it back to Humboldt for the second time since I had left the first time. Marques gave his perspective on the trip, "it was fun and exciting since I got to see some new environments. Driving your mom's car on the back of that truck was a trip. Niggas was frying on acid through the mountains. It was like a bunch of young kids on a road trip and we were out of control. (He laughs) We were smoking weed and getting high, as we always call it, traveling and takin' trips. Humboldt was dope, except for the movie theatre. When I woke up, everyone was running around the theatre portraying the roles of "Grease."

I got a hold of Cynthia, the one who flew me out to Chicago to her sister's wedding; I was in love with that girl. Unfortunately, she was a nymphomaniac and every time we were apart for any length of time, she had to have sex with somebody. I had asked her to marry me, and she told me that she loved me and would love to marry me, but that she had messed up again. I lost my mind! And females had problems with me after that. I can say that she messed it up for the rest, until I grew up enough to realize that wasn't going to benefit me in the long run.

You know it is funny, when I left for Humboldt, my mom had told me not to trust women; she said she knew because she is one. She said that women are evil. Well obviously, I learned that lesson the hard way, like most. And there were plenty examples of exactly that which my mom talked about. There was one time and one female that I can't omit, her name is Jennifer. She and I dated for a while, and I would say we were close. I guess we got too close as when we started to grow apart and I realized I didn't have the same feelings I previously had for her, she flipped out on me. I went back to my old ways and started seeing another female while Jennifer was kind of staying with Marques and I at the time. So, one night she was at the house while I was out and about, and she called me crying. She asked me to come to the house as she wanted to talk to me.

It was an **ambush**! As I walked in the door, she used mace on me and took my keys and stole my vehicle. I later found out that she went to Las Vegas and eventually she made her way back with the vehicle. This was the straw that broke the camel's back as previously there were a couple of other physical altercations. Although I cared about her at some point, I can't deny that she was crazy! Suffice it to say, we parted ways and even though we met in passing a few times, I couldn't look at her the same. She played me, disrespected me, and had me looking like a fool. Now that I reflect, I realize now how much responsibility I must take in the situation. I learned that lesson the hard way. (It really was kind of funny, only in retrospect) I also later learned that my mother wasn't entirely correct in her assessment of all women. There is good and evil in all people, and it may have been the story of Eve (Adam and Eve) she could have been referring to, yet we must discern and judge for ourselves, the potential evil within people.

Back to the Humboldt stop before the final leg of our trip to Seattle. We had a couple of days there and I saw some old schoolmates; we partied and made our way on the final trek of our travels on this trip. We finally made it to Washington and saw where my mom, Josiah, Amber, and Amanda would be living. The next day, the rest of us flew back to L.A. and so began another chapter, when we touched back down, we had 4230 W. Adams, Apartment 102 to ourselves. This turned out to be a blessing and a curse. Even though we were only there for eight more months, it's hard to believe to this day all that happened at that place. Silas was sixteen, I was twenty-one, and Marques was twenty-three. Silas talks about how, "As a teenager, I was able to talk to Marques, talk to Franco and tell them exactly what was going on with me in my life, about girls. I was able to be real with my shit." Silas laughs and resumes, "I didn't know the game yet. I remember I had a summer job at the Department of Water and Power (DWP) and I used to come up the hill in my orange jumpsuit. We used to talk and smoke and chill out. And I would ask questions like you would a father figure, cause these niggas, the group overall were like father figures to a nigga. 'Cause I didn't really have that I only had a bunch of mis-direction."

We were young and the home that my brother and I grew up in was now our bachelor pad. We grew weed in the downstairs closet, hosted neighborhood hangouts, and threw parties. I'll never forget this one party... the "blunts" (cigar split, tobacco taken out and filled with weed) were being sparked (lit) and passed. The water cooler was filled with "jungle juice" (a mixture of Rum, Vodka, pineapple juice and Kool Aid) that particular night got a little crazy when a couple of "hood heads" (neighborhood regulars) got drunk and a little rowdy. Overall, it was a hell of a night.

Marques' recollection of 4230 was, "it was the party house, like "Animal House" in the hood. It was always poppin, drinking and smoking, there were oodles of 40-ounce bottles out on the patio. Me and this nigga were like Method Man and Redman on the movie "How High." That's how it was every day, how high. Niggas from the neighborhood would come by to our spot, because we were living, living it up and having fun and enjoying life."

Silas made a point to remind me where we spent our time before we ended up with our own spot, if it was even for only a temporary amount of time, "you have to think back, Marques was living with his mom and we used to smoke out the room and she used to complain and there used to be multiple guests coming over and there were all type of things going on. But that was Marques' room. It was a respect level..." get the fuck out of my room! We chillin', what the fuck..." Marques would just snap and just go off. We would be in there smoked out and there would be pounds of weed. His cousins or whoever would be coming thru and sellin' dope... There was always a situation, but that room was a definite sanctuary. And when we were on the stairs hangin', that was a good spot since we could oversee the hood, it was like a tower."

I remember when we hung the "mic" (microphone) from the staircase, hooked it to the house stereo and that became our sound booth. All the neighborhood "wannabes" (fakers) would come through to get their practice by "freestylin'" or "battling."

One night we were hanging on the porch and a SUV was slowly driving towards us on a side street off Adams Boulevard. They had their lights off, which is usually a sign that they were on the creep. Two of the YG's (Young Gangsters) saw it coming a mile away and told us to turn off the porch and house lights. Of course, they were holding (had guns on them). Just as the SUV started to turn the corner onto Adams Boulevard, the two YG's pulled their straps (guns), ran onto the sidewalk to get closer, and they lit up (shot at) the SUV before they could get their guns out. The SUV turned the corner and slowly rolled up and onto the sidewalk and came to a stop. None of us stuck around to see the outcome and we later found out that the driver was killed, and his passenger ran away. The police never came by to question us. We were not sure if they questioned the neighbors or if they did and they just didn't say or see anything. The shots were right in from of the apartment building and could be clearly heard. We thought if they did question the neighbors, maybe since they knew who hung with us in our apartment, they may have been too scared to say anything for fear of retaliation.

We stayed there for about eight months, at which point the property management company did their due diligence to get us out of there. We didn't pay rent most of the time we were there. Come to find out that my mom took my name off the lease when I left for Humboldt. When I came back and before she left for Seattle Washington, she didn't put me back on the lease. With the help of legal aid, I was able to get us another month before we had to get out and avoided getting an eviction on my record. While unfortunately for Moms she got an eviction on her record since obviously, she didn't show up for court from Seattle. This initial experience became the first of many dealings with landlords and the housing authority court system. You must know your rights. While we were there, I did take a detour to Northridge California and Cal State University of Northridge. I spent almost a whole semester there as I was told it had one of the highest Chicano populations and had a strong MECHA chapter and had Rudy Acuna. From what I heard, he taught at UC Santa Barbara and was fired based on his political beliefs, he sued the university and won and eventually left anyway. He is one of this country's most prominent Chicano studies professors. I was blessed to have one of his classes focused on Mexican American literature of the twentieth century. The population was there, but not of the same mind set. The MECHA chapter was there, but too militant and closed minded for my taste. And the music scene was extremely saturated. I stayed in an apartment off campus with a female who I met with Marques at an underground house party at UCLA. I lived there off and on until the "Northridge Quake" (earthquake) of 1993. After that incident, I never went back, and it was a good thing that I wasn't there that day as that apartment had some structural damage. This was another example of God's presence in my life before I knew it.

*C*HAPTER 13

(1994) *Atlanta's Outkast released its first album, marking the move away from coast-centric hip-hop and officially putting the south on the map. Notorious B.I.G.'s "Ready to Die" featured the single "Big Poppa" and gained much publicity for Bad Boy Entertainment. Suge Knight insulted Puffy on stage at the Source Awards, publicly sparking East vs. West Coast tension between Bad Boy and Death Row Records.*

The next move was not premeditated, and completely unexpected. It was always about the hustle, a hook up and about who you know. Marques started talking to our neighbor I had known for years. I was close with their daughter, and they had their problems like any other family. Their daughter had moved out and got married and started her own family. The man of the house was having his issues with drugs and his wife and ended up going back to their homeland. (Nicaragua) The wife/women of the house (Carmen) and her three smaller children stayed in the home. I believe that she had her sister living with them at the time, as well. Marques, as he has always done, got friendly with Carmen and her sister. He got us invited over for some food and drinks. We finally had to get out of 4230 West Adams Boulevard, Apartment 102 completely. We kind of just moved next door. We didn't sleep there every night, and we didn't keep all our stuff there. We still spent most of our time out on the block, hustling.

(Black & Brown Movement song "It's such a crime")

"This melody should be a felony; this baseline will rape minds
This drumbeat will open rap sheets, this rhythm got you 25
to life livin,
Repentance is your sentence, case closed,
Evidence, oh yeah, they lace those,
Take this tempo, pora jemplo, this sound collage,
Yours is garbage, kept in the garage,
This music is a hustle, tapping on your head like Nipsy Russell,
These measures like my freedom I treasure,
These notes will have you behind bars, no audio pleasure,
My volume meter floats afar,
My rhyming with timing, stops at its midi marker,
We'll have you in the middle of downtown's Parker Center,
It's such a crime!"

There were a lot of characters either from or who "kicked it" (hung out) in our hood.

There was this one kat that seemed to always gravitate toward us, and we'll call him "G." His mother lived in the hood, which is why he was always around, but he was from another Blood gang. I'll never forget G; he was crazy, and his MO (modus operandi) was house "liks." (gigs/jobs) He would find his way into your house, day, or night, with you in it and would come out with something of value, even if it had to be from your pockets. One time while we were still at Carmen's, in broad day light, he took her thirty-six-inch Sony TV when we weren't there. That thing had to weigh at least over one hundred pounds and he somehow got it over her patio wall. We couldn't ever live that one down either, as she had a suspicion that it was somebody associated with us.

There was the time that we drank a gallon of "Remy Martin." (Cognac) I was vomiting for two days straight. Another time he convinced me to drive him and "D" (another homie) to Whittier, before we ever lived there, as him and D handled a few house liks. (burglaries/home invasions) The lure was a cut of the profits, but the only thing they came up on that night was some costume jewelry and a couple of VCRs. That didn't work out so well and I never did it again.

At the time, without a job and just losing our own roof over our head for the last eight months, times were rough. Marques made a call to one of his "big brother figures," to get us a plugged into the drug trafficking game. It started with a greyhound bus trip to Saint Louis Missouri from Hollywood California. The first time was terrifying. There were two of us, one sat on the back of the bus and the other sat near the front of the bus. One of us would place the package on the overhead luggage racks somewhere in the middle of the bus. We would act like we met on the trip at a stop on the way to Missouri.

When we finally would get to our destination, one of us would get the package as we exited the bus. Springfield Missouri, just outside of Saint Louis, was a stop that would frighten me extremely. As we rolled up to the bus stop, you could see about nine D.E.A. agents with two dogs. As soon as we get off the bus, the agents and dogs checked the bus for drugs as we were filed into the station. See, the biggest problem to arise on this trip, was the course of events that were about to unfold at this station. I was warned about Springfield Missouri but wasn't warned that my ticket had the same name as the other guy that was on the trip. After searching the bus and obviously not finding anything, the DEA agents made their way into the terminal. While I sat at one end of the terminal, the other guy sat at the other end. I was wearing athletic gear and reading a book and listening to a Walkman. Of course, I had to play a role that convinced I was the farthest thing from a drug smuggler. So, as I witnessed through my peripheral vision, the other guy was getting interviewed by one of the DEA agents. I had to keep my composure. I watched the other guy hand over his ticket to the agent and saw him pull out his ID. The agent matched the ID to the ticket, and all was well with him. Just as the agent had handed back the ID and the ticket, another agent stepped up to me. The semi-interrogation began. "Where are you going and where are you coming from? What's your name and where's your ticket?" I answered all his questions without hesitation. It's on the bus, would like me to go get it? He paused for a minute and said not to worry about it.

Now let's recap at one point, two agents stood in the middle of the bus terminal. After talking to the other guy and myself, holding both of our tickets, with the other guy's name on them. I'm sure they realized that we were both leaving from the same starting point and going to the same destination. The difference is that the other guy had the ID to match. That sequence of events, I'll never forget. First was that agent who asked me why I was going to Saint Louis. I told him I was on a recruiting trip to the University of Saint Louis. I believe the combination of that as well as the attire I was wearing and the false confidence and composure I was displaying, all contributed to me getting out of the situation. (In reality, I was scared "shitless" (to death) God of course was the real reason. And of course, the second thing I'll never forget was when he asked me for my ID. He asked me this after asking me if I knew the other guy and if I knew we had the same name. He explained that the tickets showed that we were leaving the same place, heading to the same place. He asked me whether I was aware of that. Again, I said no, without hesitation and with full confidence. Obviously, the fact that they didn't find anything on the bus made it easier for the agent to let me go without getting the ID off that bus. Now the reason they didn't find anything on the bus was due to the way it was packaged. There were two kilos of cocaine, one in each speaker of a portable radio. (Boom box) The kilos were in their own plastic bags and then repackaged in coffee grinds and Vaseline. This would throw the scent off the dogs.

When we arrive at the downtown Saint Louis bus station, one of us would grab the radio and this time it was me. After grabbing my bag, I would call a cab to a central location (hub) When we would get to the "spot," (location) they would crack open the radio and begin the process. That included unwrapping the kilos and dividing the amount that was to be cooked into "crack cocaine."

We stayed in the "Lou" (Saint Louis) for about a week, while the money was made. I was taken to different "spots" (houses) where the cooking took place. I was taken to the neighborhoods where the "crack" was sold. I was taken to the businesses that served as fronts. The businesses were a liquor store, a dry cleaner, and an office cleaning service. I remember when we were in one of the neighborhoods where the product was sold. I saw some "tags" (graffiti) on the walls of the abandoned buildings. A couple of "tags" were "Inglewood Family," "Long Beach," "Rollin' 60's" and "8 trays." These are all gangs from Southern California, Los Angeles County area. We would laugh at the locals and remind them that they didn't even know where these places were. I remember getting invited to a "basement party." Every house had a basement, and this one was deep (lots of people) The DJ was "jammin'" (playing a lot of good music) and the lights were flashing, and someone jumped on the Mic. Next thing I know, I'm in the thick of a freestyle battle. Later on, I found out that I had battled "Nelly," one of if not the best MC to come out of the "Lou" (Saint Louis) As I exited that basement, that day, I was given "mad props" (Lots of accolades) on the way out for holding my own against "Nelly."

There were a couple of other vivid memories from my time spent in the "Lou." The younger brother of our main connect was appointed to be my guide/security, his name was "Bootsy." When I first met him, I was sitting out in the car waiting to be introduced when a couple of local females were walking by, one of them looked at me and stopped and said, "My name is Peaches, what's yours?" She said that she knew I wasn't a local and was from out of town. I remember playing basketball at one of their more infamous parks; I forget the name of it. There were a few of the locals who were talking out loud about me being a "fed." (police officer) Obviously this was due to my white complexion and them not being used to someone with my complexion in their environment, unless they were a cop. I was having a good game and I think this made them even angrier and caused one of them to approach me in a hostile manor. They all knew Bootsy but didn't know that I was with him, and he was on my team. So, Bootsy stepped up and let them all know that if they had a problem with me, they would have a problem with him. The game commenced and of course we won.

There was another time when Bootsy took me to a "Juke Joint" (a social bar/club usually found down south and sometimes in the mid-west) in East St. Louis. This area is comparable to that of South-Central Los Angeles regarding being the roughest part of the city, rough in terms of crime, drugs, and violence. This Juke Joint was small; there was the bar of course, a small dance floor and a couple of pool tables. I was at one of the pool tables watching Bootsy get his hustle on while observing the only other non-Black person in the joint who was at the bar with a woman on each side of him. He was an older white gentleman who looked like he was "tricking" (spending money on women in the hopes that they would sleep with you) on the ladies he was with at the bar.

I was getting those same looks and hearing the whispers about me being a fed again. Bootsy finished his game, took his earnings, and got me out of there, just to be safe. By the time we left, there was a whole new adventure waiting for us at the airport.

When we made it to the airport, the trip was over as we had the money to transport back. Of course, the "dough" (money) was also in the speakers of that "boom box" (portable radio) When me and Marques walked down the main isle of Saint Louis' main airport, carrying our bags and that boom box, airport police and/or DEA (Drug Enforcement Agency) agents surrounded us on both sides. They pulled us apart and I remember the first question asked was, "are you transporting large sums of currency?" The second question was, "can I search your bag?" Of course, I said yes. On the other side, where they pulled Marques to, I could hear him yelling, "are you a harassing me because I'm Black?" A minute later, they let us both go, and we caught our flight home. Of course, there was $50,000.00 in the speakers of the boom box. And of course, it couldn't be detected as the magnets of the speakers masked the magnetic strips in the $20's $50's and $100.00 bills. (not to mention the fact that there were a good number of $10- and $5-dollar bills that didn't have magnetic strips) When we got back into town (LA) and we touched down, we got the boom box to its rightful owner.

This got us about $5,000.00 a piece for a week's work and just as we were getting used to that kind of money, Marques came to me one day and said that God had told him that it was time to stop. I told him that I was not going to argue with God, so we stopped.

Marques also told one of our other boys (who was also trafficking) about his dream.

However, he said he couldn't stop as he had a kid on the way. Unfortunately, he went again and got "popped" (arrested) and ended up spending three years in a federal prison. The only good thing about the situation was the fact that he was still in California when he got caught, if he had made it over to Arizona, he would have had a lot longer sentence. One thing we made sure of was that we spent that "blood" money as soon as we got it. We knew that we were contributing to the genocide of our peoples and that money would burn in our hands and in our pockets. We bought clothes and shoes and went to concerts and threw parties. We did whatever we could to get rid of that money as fast as we got it, knowing the whole time that we were dead wrong.

When we first started going out of town, the "kat" that was sending us out of town, helped us get an apartment in Whittier. He was like a big brother to Marques. So, we ended up getting out of the hood and ended up getting our own place again. Keep in mind, I still had my little brother with me. I tried getting him enrolled in high school out in Whittier, but that didn't work out. I ended up getting on the "county" (welfare) to bring in some food stamps and extra funds after we stopped going out of town. For some reason because the case was in his name, my brother thought he was supposed to be getting all the money.

The final Endeavour with "G" (mentioned earlier) came when we moved to Whittier, the first night we were there he took Silas with him on a house lick, they came back with a stack of cash. When he finally told us where and how they got the money, Marques and I were pissed as it was the first night at this new apartment and in a new town. G came with us to Whittier because he was on the run from the law and was on the list of "America's Most Wanted." It was also a popular TV show at the time. The reason G was on the run was due to a (guess what) house lick he did with another infamous gangster from our hood, his name was "P." That dude was infamous due to major "work" he put in. The most infamous story about him was the time he was shot with an "UZI" sub-machine gun, it was seventeen times in the back with 45-caliber bullets, while he was running away. And he lived! Whenever those two got together, it was bad news. It was being reported that they had performed a house invasion on an Asian household, and not only did they rob these folks while they were home, but they also raped two of the women in the house. G ended up turning himself in as the law kept harassing his mother and he didn't want us to get caught up for harboring a fugitive. They ended up catching up with P and they both got triple life.

The year plus we spent in Whittier was interesting, the two apartments we lived in, the money we had coming in and didn't know how to manage. Marques talked about the apartment complex we lived in called the "Vikings" apartments, "they were fun when me and this nigga were going out of town, I was gone one week, and he was gone the other. We had cheese! We lived next door to a liquor store and every day we went to the store and at that time we were drinking this special brew that Miller had. I think it was Amber Ale or something. We were drinking those, and smoking blunts of "fire" out of those Behringer cigars that were about $3 each. We were smoking blunts before "Redman" came out in the "High Times" magazine talking about how to roll a blunt. We were so crazy, we made our own drink, we called it a Bongeritas. We used bong water and Tequila, sounds gross, I know. We lived the life at 4230, but we really lived the life at the Vikings in Whittier because we didn't do nothing but have fun, every day, all day."

Obviously, the situation changed when we decided to stop going out of town. We had no income and went back to hustling for a while. We partied a lot and there were a lot of girls who came and went. We sold some drugs and took some and my little brother was exposed to it all. We were still lost in the land of the lost. He did everything we did, to keep up with us. One night we were drinking, and partying and little brother took it too far. We were at the first apartment complex we stayed at in Whittier, which was only a couple of a complexes down. Little bro stumbled down from that complex to the new apartment we were staying at. We lived upstairs and had those plate glass windows just next to the front door. So, he crawled up the stairs and broke about four or five plates to get into the apartment, even though he had the keys. When we realized that he was missing from the party, we walked over to our apartment and as we got to our complex, we spotted vomit in the walkway and some on the stairs. When we get to the door, we saw that the glass plates had been broken. When we opened the door, there was more vomit on the carpet trailing to the bathroom. There he was, hugging the toilet.

We were disappointed and at that point, I don't think he was too concerned about that. We asked him why he broke the glass when he had the key. He was drunk and couldn't even talk. We helped clean him up and told him that he was going to have to clean up his mass. He seemed to be starting to sober up out of nowhere and he decided he wanted to cuss us out. We looked at each other like, "isn't he the one that's wrong?"

Eventually he decided he was going to leave and felt like he had to mention the county (welfare) situation on his way out. After realizing that he was more sober than drunk and that he was talking shit (trash) to me, who he begged to let him stay with, I decided to let him go.

Shortly after that situation, we ended up leaving that apartment and making our way back to the hood. Unfortunately, we had to go back to Marques' mom's house. Of course, this meant back to that environment. Marques continued to hustle (sold marijuana) while I went back to school. We had made a pact that we would never again sell anything other than weed. We still stayed under the same roof, but slightly went in two different directions. Both actions were necessary as I didn't have a job or income other than financial aid, which was never enough. Caught in the middle of all of this was Silas, my little brother who we ran back into in the hood.

Around this time, a family friend of the Jones', the McDaniels' showed back up after some years of being out of the loop. There was Father Greg, Mother Stephanie, three sons: "O", Chris and Santiago. There were also two sisters,

Sasha and Misa and I got close to Misa who was close to my age, and we began dating. Misa and I started going to school together, and I ended up moving in with her and her family. I didn't leave on good terms since Marques, and I got into a huge fight. He was upset that while he was in jail for a few months for gun possession (remember he had been shot before) I was getting close to Misa and not doing much else. He was also upset that since I decided to go back to school that I wasn't hustling while he was gone and there was nothing for him to come back to, money or product. Silas was again caught in limbo as I was spending more time with Misa, I just left him to fend for himself to an extent. So, we had a blowout not unlike others in the past except for the fact that this one went to the highest of extremes and would no doubt take that much longer to bounce back from if at all or ever. I mean I told him that he was the reason that his girlfriend/love of his life was killed, and he told me that I was the reason that I didn't have my daughter and that her mother took off with her. In the interim, I left Silas at Connie's (Marques's mom) and Marques stayed and tried his best to hold it together. Looking back at it now and as I have many times since, I realized the selfish decision I had made, chasing love "sucker for love" as it's been called. When I moved in with Misa, Silas made his way back up to Seattle and he ended up finishing high school, graduating, and getting his diploma.

That whole situation, although a strenuous one, may have been a blessing in disguise for Silas. It motivated him to do something for himself and he went to Mid-City where he and Josiah had attended to a certain grade along with myself and he talked to the school secretary who knew our family very well since I went there, and our mother had worked there for some time as well. Her name is Curly, and she was a school mother figure to all the students who attended Mid-City Alternative Magnet school and to all those who met her. Curly knew that Silas hadn't been to school in a couple of years and knew he only had one chance/year left to finish it and make it happen. So, she offered to help by giving him some of the credits that he needed up to his senior year that allowed him to go to high school in Seattle, complete his senior year and graduate.

Silas said, "The whole thing I was dreading was going up there and living with my mom and Rick Compton. I had to live up under them and their rules. The best thing for me to do was to skate and be out of the house as much as possible. That's when I got a job at Burger King. I just remember dealing with these new people and having sex with girls in cars and living with these people with a whole new mindset. When you go to Seattle, they have a different mindset than LA (Los Angeles) they are all free. These kids up there had cars, they had money, they had weed, and we had fun. And after all that I had been through, I graduated, and I walked across the stage. It was a blessing to me, and I couldn't believe it, my mom couldn't believe it and Rick couldn't believe it. He was hatin' like, "this nigga actually walked across the stage, after all this." He even told me later that he couldn't believe I did when I hadn't done shit the two years before. But he didn't know that I had done a lot of living, with my brothers. I fucked with and learned a lot from Marques, from G, from Franco. We were out on the block, grinding. My mom dumped me, hello! I didn't really have anything else to do. But I came back to Seattle, and I graduated, and they looked at me like, "how did you do this?"

Misa's family lived in the hills known as the "Jungles," like hazard projects there was one way in and pretty much one way out. They weren't projects, but a community of apartments. It was infamous for housing the same "Blood" gang that was in my hood "BPS" (Black P Stone) They sold drugs and battled any rival gang that had the heart to enter the "jungle." I am not here to glorify the lifestyle, but it is what it is, and it was what it was. I don't condone the behavior, but I understand it. Silas talked about how he managed while I was living with Misa and her parents in the "J's," "I was pretty much on the streets. If I didn't come back up the hill at a certain time, it was lights out, cause Connie (Marques and Nikki's mother) don't play! It's a wrap! I had to figure out where I was going to live and what I was going to do. I was a young nigga in the game trying to figure out my goal and my path. I figured the best situation for me would be to find a female and I found one and she lived in the "Jungles,"and she had two kids and she was thirty-something. She kinda light weight took me in, she was my "go to," which meant I had a spot to go to."

This was a temporary situation as Misa and I began to have issues in our relationship, which began to be strained while I was living with her and her parents and did not have a job at the time. I finally got a job with the "Warehouse Records" store. Shortly after that, Misa's older sister Sasha (who I was always close to) helped me find a studio apartment down the street from her. She knew the struggles her sister, and I were having. I remember coming home (Misa's parents' house) and Misa's ex-boyfriend was there, who I had heard way too much about to that point. That was my sign, as if I needed anymore.

$\mathscr{C}$HAPTER 14

(1995) *After going public with his HIV status, N.W.A.'s Eazy-E died of AIDS at the age of thirty-one. Rapper 2Pac signed on with Death Row after Suge Knight paid his bail. Queen Latifah received a Grammy for her hit single "U.N.I.T.Y.")*

I ended up moving to that studio apartment if you could even call it that. It was a fixer upper to move in and there was a bunch of trash and major plumbing problems, but it was my own. By this time, Marques and I began hanging out again, and he was having problems at his mom's house, so I told him to move in with me. This began a whole new era.

The management company that was renting out these shacks was charging $200.00 a month, and that only lasted about three months until another company bought the land and there was a legal battle that left us in limbo for about five months, when we didn't have to pay anything. Not that these shacks were worth anything anyway. In the months that we stayed there, I was working at the Warehouse Records and learning about the music industry, business of music retail and was making numerous connections. By the time I moved into this "spot," (place) we were selling weed, while the neighbor across from us sold crack. Although we never "gang banged" (became members of and represented a gang in negative and illegal activities) we did associate with the "Blood" and Latino gangs from the neighborhood we grew up in. The neighborhood we moved to in Inglewood California had its own Blood and Latin gangs. After they found out that we were selling weed in their neighborhood and our neighbor was selling crack, he was also from a Blood gang, and they didn't appreciate us making money in their territory. Working at the Warehouse Records gave me the business background I needed to understand the music industry. Our warehouse/product manager was already established and associated with even more established Hip Hop artists at that time. (He was the DJ/producer of the group "Black Forrest" and they were under a bigger group. "Visionaries".) I got close with him as well as the upper management of the store and this introduced me to established artists managers, A&R's, producers, promoters, and distributors. I also had up and coming (underground) artists who would ask if they could pass promotional materials and post the same in our store and if we would play their music as well. I remember artists like "2MEX," "Ralph M the Mexican," "Funk Doobiest," and "Montell Jordan." I remember meeting and getting to know local radio DJ's and street teams from stations like 92.3 "The Beat." I was getting invited to industry parties and events and it was V.I.P. status all the way and backstage passes to shows like the "Pharcyde." There was full access to venues like the House of Blues. This is when I really started getting in tuned with the craft. We started hitting up the underground spots and started making rounds on the freestyle circuit. The few main spots at the time were "Project Blowed," "Elements," and "Unity." There were so many spots and battles and artists who came and went and who were almost all intertwined as I will touch on later within this story. Josiah, my youngest brother was having issues up north with my mom and her husband, so he came down to visit me for about a week. We ended up going to a Laker game while he was down (Marques sacrificed his ticket so Josiah could go). It was the last Laker game ever played in the then Great Western Forum. There was an event at my job that was called the "Block Party," there was a stage for performances and promotional booths. It was a big event for us. I remember "Xzibit" and the "Luniz" and a couple of other R & B acts who performed as they were top artists at the time. I introduced Josiah to all the peoples I knew, including a couple of street promoters. Little did I know what that would lead to. We had a good time, and I was taking him back to the airport when we stopped at a gas station, I went to pay for the gas and when I came back to the car, it was up against the brick wall in front of the gas pump. Josiah was in the passenger seat and had a look of panic on his face, "I hit the stick shift." I laughed at him and the little scratch on the hood and we continued.

So back to the issue we had at our new spot in Inglewood with the local gangs. We would come home to threats on our door as the tension began to build. The height of the tension broke out into a full blown, "wild west" show down. This happened after the local Blood gang "Inglewood Family" sent a couple of their "baby" (younger) members over to our neighborhood shack. They broke into our neighbor's place and were looking for the drugs and or money and found neither as well as that gun that was under his couch. When he came home to find these youngsters in his spot, he went straight for his gun that they had missed and chased them out of his shack, pointing the gun at them. We all stood and watched as we knew that they would be back.

All this action had happened earlier that evening and sure enough later that night, they came back. Our neighbor was waiting with his gun and had sent them off with a couple of warning shots as they hung across the street at a gas station parking lot. So, when they came back, that's where they stopped. We spotted them as they arrived and so did our neighbor, our neighbor stepped out in the open and gestured to them as if he was asking them what they wanted. They immediately pulled out a handgun and began shooting. A good thing was that they didn't know how to shoot. The bullets were flying, hitting the side of the building and Marques' car that was in the driveway. Our neighbor (whose name was Ace) who also knew how to shoot a gun was able to drive back two guns, with one.

Just before this event had taken place, Marques had met a female who just moved to the states from Australia. Her name is Donna, and she was there that night, what a culture shock huh? Not too long after that happened, we were out of there. Marques and Donna got closer, and she decided she wanted to help us move out of the hood. We ended up in East Los Angeles. It was a garage and pool house converted, but it was better and bigger than the shack in Inglewood we eventually ended up naming the "pit." (This became the theme of every spot we moved to and resided in) The converted garage was configured in an interesting way, the main garage area was insulated and carpeted and used as the main living area/living room. There was a staircase leading up to a loft and the kitchen area, a bathroom, and another room. The pool was just outside the dwelling and of course there was the main house in front of this property. The property was located at the top of a hill and in the heart of East L.A.

Before we left the "Pit," (Inglewood) I was still working at Wherehouse Records and Nik came to the job and told me that I would be her husband. She said God told her. This was surprising to me since she had seen me at my worst, after Cynthia. She saw me at her house with other females, with hickies (red spots on your neck, from someone sucking on it) on my neck. She saw me in a car with one female, while another walked up to the car to confront me. I am not saying this to brag, just the opposite, to show how lost I was at the time. When we were younger, she wouldn't give me the time of day. And now she was approaching me. One night she had dinner at her house and her mom, her brother Marques, her son Jalen and I were all there. After dinner was over, Nik whispered to me, telling me to come back to her house later that night. I always had a crush on her since we were younger. So, when the opportunity presented itself, I didn't hesitate to take advantage of it. We made love that night, not just sex and it was special, not just because it was the first time. Nik ended up having a tubal pregnancy that had to be terminated.

We began dating off and on for some months. I was not ready to commit or grow up or give up (being a dog) what I was doing before we began dating. I caused a lot of drama and hurt and pain for Nik. One of the times we broke up, we had "break-up sex," in her bedroom closet. That is how we conceived our first son Juwan. I was not the best father I could be to my son the first few years of his life. Nik and I were not together, and I had not yet gotten the epiphany. Nik held it down as she has always done. She came to me about fathering another child, she didn't want another "baby's Daddy" and I didn't want another man in my son's life, so I agreed. Nik already had Jalen and Juwan and she wanted a girl. This is how we got our third son Josiah (yes, I named him after my brother R.I.P.)

Josiah was born five weeks pre-mature and saved my wife's life in the process. Nik had "walking pneumonia" and him inducing labor allowed the doctors to catch it, deliver Josiah via sea section and treat her for the illness. Her pregnancy was rough as she developed gestational diabetes. Josiah was born with a hole in his heart and his first year was tuff, starting with three weeks in NICU. (Neo-natal Intensive Care Unit) Every time he had caught a little cold we ended up at the hospital. By the time he turned one years old, he had his second surgery and thank God, this one was successful. Nik and I got so much closer going through all of that together and I grew up in the process. When I was young, I always said that I would look around my world when I turned thirty and whoever had been down with me, that's who I would marry. It was Nik, I just happened to be thirty-one instead. She had put up with so much. She was the best mother to my children that I could ask for and I had always loved her; it just took me loving myself enough to realize it. We ended up getting married, and we had our baby girl, Jazmyn Catherine Rene Brocks ("Princessa")

We ended up having problems with our landlord at the time and only lived at that place for about eight months. As I mentioned previously, we ran into drama a few times with landlords and the courts. Connie (Marques' moms) found us another place in the East LA area. This new place was nice, two bedrooms and a loft. It was also on the hilltop just behind California State University of Los Ang Angeles. After we moved in, we found out that the house was a historical monument. It seems that in 1969 when the Beatles came to America, they stayed at that house. There were eight years of memories, some bad and mostly good. Before moving to East L.A. and at some limbo stage, there was the incident that landed me in jail for the first time,

I was still working at the Warehouse Records at the time, I had just gotten paid that day, and my brother Josiah was with me. He was there as he had made his way back down and moved in with me. I went to the shoe store as it was Fourth of July weekend and I had $500.00 in my pocket. I was trying on some sneakers and was trying to decide whether to buy them. There was a rack of cubbyholes near the front door entrance where I had placed my backpack. I remembered another time when Marques and I went to the same shoe store at another location and Marques pulled off the "switcheroo" successfully. It was a pair of boots that he was wearing that he switched with a similar pair of boots. I guess I was a little tempted to try it as I tried on a similar pair of black sneakers compared to the ones I came in with. I remember that I thought I was going to get away with it instead of paying with the cash I had in my pocket. I ended up crossing the line (I of course knew nothing about) where the security guard saw I was still wearing the new shoes. The security guard immediately grabbed me and told me to put my hands behind back. I attempted to tell him (make the excuse) that I was going for my checkbook, but he explained that I had crossed the line.

It all turned bad when I refused to put my hands behind my back and the guard decided he would force my hands behind my back. As I continued to struggle, the guard pulled out his mace and sprayed it in my eyes. I reacted and started swinging my fists. I couldn't see but felt a few of those punches connect with the head of the guard. I remember the guard being quite a bit bigger and taller than me. My sight came back a little and I remember running past the guard, headed for the door. Another employee tried blocking the door and I remember hitting him and seeing a little light of day before I was tripped up just outside of the shoe store. At that point, I had the guard and the other employee over me with a barrage of punches. As I said, my brother Josiah was with me and saw the whole thing. I could hear him in the background yelling, "Leave my brother alone!" Somehow, I was able to squirm my way out of my shirt they were holding on to and began running down the main street of Crenshaw Boulevard. I had "just below my shoulder" length hair that was all over the place. I had two black and red and puffy burning eyes and no shirt on while running down Crenshaw Boulevard. Baldwin Hills were over to the left and that was my destination, until "Super Citizen" decided he wanted to play "Starsky" or was it "Hutch?" I'll never forget, it was a bright cherry red EL Camino, and it turned right in front of me, and I rolled over its hood. When I rolled over the hood of that vehicle, I rolled into the parking lot of a smaller shopping center and into some oil and what I had hoped was some dog shit and not human feces. "Captain Community" (A.K.A Captain Save a Ho) got out of his 'hater-mobile," took off his belt and used it as "makeshift" handcuffs. I was done and completely out of it. By this time the "rent-a-cop" from the shoe store, had caught his fat ass up with the real handcuffs. I was taken to the nearest hospital since I was having trouble breathing, and then the 77th division station, put in a holding cell until they could get a "black and white" to take me downtown. By the time it was all over, my hair was a mess and all over the place, my eyes were red and blackened, I was beat up and exhausted and I was filthy and smelled like shit. This was not how I had imagined this Fourth of July weekend to start off and I had not expected to be arrested for the first time. Again, it's funny now in retrospect.

When I got to booking, they took my personal items, right down to my hair tie and threw me in another holding cell. As I was sitting there, I looked up and guess who I saw? "Pops the dope fiend, high off his dope, who doesn't know the meaning of water nor soap." (Some of you may get that reference?) Pops was getting fingerprinted and when I was able to get his attention, he yelled "that's my son, that's my son." The deputy jabbed him in the ribs and told him to shut up. Pops and I spent a week together in what's called the "glass house," a smaller jail facility where instead of bars it was glass/plastic that separated inmates from the halls of this facility. These were the same halls that the deputies roamed and periodically came to call roll. Pops and I have the same first and last name, so you can imagine the deputies' looks of confusion when we both answered, one black, and one looking white. There were twenty to thirty inmates per cell. I helped Pops "kick" (get through with drawls from heroin) by giving him my orange juices and requesting a bible from a deputy. I read him the book of "John," until we were shipped to the county jail.

I hadn't seen Pops in about eleven years. The last time I saw him was on a Thanksgiving Day eleven years earlier. Marques and I rolled out to find Pops at MacArthur Park, just west of downtown L.A. Through the grace of God, we found him. It was raining, and it was nighttime, and we were bringing him a plate of food. It was cold and Pops did not have a jacket. Marques had a jacket in the back of his car, and he begrudgingly allowed me to give it to him.

The L.A. County jail is in downtown Los Angeles; this is where they separated us into two different gang models. I was in the 9400 module and Pops was in 9500. I was in "D" (Denver Row) and I ended up going through the release process three times during the month that I was there. The first time was before I made it to the 9400 modules;

I got what's called a lucky seven. This is when an inmate is randomly picked to get released before getting completely through processing, due to overcrowding. I wasn't exactly sure what it was and another inmate around me said that I was getting out. I went through that entire process for the first time, which takes an average of twenty-four hours. You get shuffled from one holding cell to a long and cold and dark hallway. When I made it to the end, I was turned back as I had traffic warrants that I had to clear up. The second time I went through the entire twenty-four-hour process when I tried to post bail, remember I had $500.00 in my pocket when I went to jail.

Now while I was in there, there were some interesting lowlights. Because I had not cleared up all the traffic warrants, they denied my bail and sent me back to general population. I was bussed/shipped from court to court, to the cities where the infractions occurred to see a judge who gave me "time served" and cleared each warrant. Some of these warrants were up to ten years old, one of them was for "jaywalking." When we had court, we were taken to an area where there were a bunch of holding cells and benches that were near the busses. They separated inmates according to the courts they were headed to. One day I bumped into a cousin of mine who I had heard was in jail for molesting who I thought was his daughter, come to find out was another minor female that was living with him. I found out later that he didn't even do it. He was totally spaced out and he didn't even recognize me, and we grew up together.

If I'm not mistaken, I was headed for Inglewood court. I remember on the bus ride there; everyone was buzzing about the small man in about his late forties or early fifties. He was being transported in the "cage" (a special seat directly behind the driver that was literally caged off) When we got to the court and were put in the holding cell, there was this huge dude who was walking around rather irritated. I overheard him talking to another inmate and was telling him very adamantly that he was getting harassed by the other inmates about being a child molester. He was saying that he must have the same name as the molester since that was what everyone was going by. He then turned his attention to the small older gentleman that was in the cage on the bus. He walked over to him and asked him for his name and what he was in for. The small man did not answer and seemed to be very nervous. The huge dude began searching the small man's pockets for his "pink slip," that was a piece of paper that every inmate carried with them on their way to court, it shows your name and what you're in for. When the huge dude pulled it out of his pocket looked and he said, "it's you!" The small man had the same name as the huge dude, and he was the "Inglewood Molester."

I had a little white towel, and he asked if he could use it, I wasn't about to refuse. He took the towel and wrapped it around the small man's head and tossed him to the ground. He began to "stomp" him out. (kick someone when they're down) The huge dude then told everyone that if they didn't "stomp" him out too, that they would have to deal with him. He asked, "Do you have kids?" So of course, I got a couple of kicks in. Somehow the small man was able to get up and make his way to the door and banged until a deputy opened the door, peaked into the holding cell, and asked, "Is there a problem in here?" Everyone quickly answered "No!" The deputy shut the door, and everyone commenced to stomping out the "Inglewood Molester." Ten minutes later, two deputies came in and pulled the little man out of the holding cell.

The other incident happened when I spent my first night in the 9400-gang module, and I wasn't a gang member. There was the one time when I was in Jr. High and there was someone from "18th Street" (an older and famous Mexican gang from LA), who was trying to recruit at my school. I agreed to join and the next day just before school started, they jumped me in. The initiation was them beating me up for eighteen seconds. That day we skipped school and just rode the bus (RTD Rapid Transit District) all day long and hit up (tagged) "18" on all the buses and ran from the Metro Police. When we got back to school at the end of the day, I told them to jump me out and that was the one and only day I ever gang banged.

I had top bunk and used my sneakers as a pillow as I had heard to do. The deputies call "lights out" and the only light was the one the deputies had behind their plastic enclosure where they watch the module. When the lights go out, even with the deputy's light, it was dark. It had to be about fifteen to twenty minutes after 'lights out" was called, that I heard the "thumps." I could barely see, other than some silhouettes, it was about four or five to one and I knew it was the "Surrenos" (southerners) (Mexican gang with ties to the Mexican Mafia) I had learned so much about jail life and culture and about how it works, all from the streets. And now I was seeing it firsthand. When I resided on Denver Row, I slept on the bunks, on what was called the "Freeway." It was bunks that were outside of the cells, again due to overcrowding. It really was like the movies. I was approached by the "Woods" (whites, not necessarily with the Arian Brotherhood) since they thought I was one of them. I was like, "Nah brah, I can't hang with y'all." I was approached in the showers by the Surrenos, "where you from ese?" I had to speak the best Spanish I could to convince them I wasn't some wood. "Yo soy un hombre de familia, puro respecto para Surrenos, pero yo soy Mexicano y Italiano." (translation= "I am a family man, and I respect the Surrenos, but I am Mexican and Italian") They bought it and never approached me again while I was in there. I hung out with everybody and was forced to work out (mostly push-ups and sit ups) by some huge brothas. I played spades (a hood card game) with other brothas and Mexicans. And I talked with the jail house lawyers.

The last time I ran into Pops in there, he told me that he was going "up state" (to state prison) for a year. I gave him my address and told him to write me and when he got out of prison, I told him he could stay with me. When we were in the "glass house" together, he had told me that every time he had gone to prison, when he got out, he had nowhere to go or stay and that was how he ended up back in the streets.

I'll never forget my last moments in jail. I got approached by this big brotha for my shoes, I had some decent Nike sneakers. I remember being told in the hood that this happens and what to say. He said, "hey homie what size them shoes?" I responded, "my size," as I looked him straight in the eyes.

I was told to be prepared to fight for the shoes, even if I got my ass whipped, because if I didn't, I would look like a punk and would be subject to others testing me. Again, even if I had gotten beat down, at least everyone would know I wasn't a punk. I was sweating bullets and shitting bricks, but he just looked at the shoes (they probably wouldn't have fit him) and looked at me and walked away.

There was a long row of holding cells on either side, packed like sardines. There were deputies that roamed up and down to keep order. And there was this female deputy who clearly explained that when she called our names that we had better yell out or booking number, or we would be sent to the back of the line. I guess you can imagine how loud I screamed out that number as I couldn't stand another second in that "hell hole."

*C*HAPTER 15

(1996) *"The Score," the Fugees' second release, combined hip-hop with R&B and reggae influences and became a top selling album. Foxy Brown and Lil Kim released debut albums with lyrics promoting female sexuality. After leaving a Mike Tyson fight in Las Vegas, a car containing Suge Knight and Tupac Shakur was shot at. Tupac died from his wounds days later, on September 13."*

So, a whole new era in the Movement's music started at our new location. For all the time that we spent there we were able to build up our studio (equipment) our catalog and our connects (clients, artists, conglomerates) After coming out of jail, of course I lost the job at the Warehouse Records, but I had already secured my connects and had already plugged Josiah into the world of promotions. After Silas had graduated from high school in Seattle, he made his way back down to stay with us in L.A. Eventually after Josiah was having problems with Moms' husband Rick, he came down to stay with us as well. Josiah and Silas formulated a promotional team, working for a street promotional, hustling entrepreneur by the name of Mike Nixon. (N5 Promotions)

They built themselves quite an empire. Mr. Nixon used these youngsters to promote the artists that were on the labels that were paying him. From singles to albums, from bumper stickers to posters, from autograph signings to radio interviews, from small clubs and venues to big concerts. Mr. Nixon had all these different labels as accounts and handled their street promotions for them. Mr. Nixon paid these youngsters based on what they did and proved using pictures they took of their work. Josiah learned a lot from N5 and the promotions game and he eventually broke from N5 promotions to start his own.

Josiah was able to get accounts with most of the labels he had promoted for N5. Street promotions consists of handing out promotional singles, albums, stickers, posters, "gear" (hats, t-shirts, bandanas) Anything can be used as promotional material, if it displays whatever it is that's being promoted. There are countless ways to be creative in doing this and one of my favorites is "lacing." This is a technique used first at record stores where they were called displays. When I worked at the Warehouse Records, I remember promoters came in to hit up their "displays." They made designs with them, and they were usually those mini posters where the paper stock was thicker, and this made it easier to fold and bend into different shapes that contributed to the designs, and "lacing" was born.

It was done differently by street promoters out in the streets; they would go up a city block and make sure that every telephone and light pole every bus stop and blank wall every stop light and stop sign had either a sticker or a mini poster stapled to it. When they took it to the next level, they would make picket signs and wear the gear of the artists and plenty other product, while standing outside of a show. They made sure that everyone knew who they were promoting, and it's called "gorilla marketing."

I remember Josiah and Silas coming home from a dinner with a hip-hop legend/mogul by the name of Russell Simmons. They brought back doggy bags of lobster tails and "filet minion" and a bottle of Don Perion. Josiah said that Mr. Simmons called him his best street promoter on the West Coast. (Russell Simmons is the founder of DEF JAM Records, was once manager of the legendary hip-hop group RUN-DMC) I also remember them coming home and talking about meeting artists such as "Common," "Most Def," "Talib Kwaleb," "Twista," "L.L. Cool J," "JAY-Z" and so many more. They used to bring home endless amounts of promotional gear, whether it was hats, t-shirts, sweat suits, tennis shoes or jeans. They would wear the gear as they were out promoting and these brands either sponsored them or their artists. It got to a point where they were making more money and getting so intertwined into the industry and being as young as they were, it got to their heads a little bit.

Unfortunately for them, I had to be the one to bust their bubble. They took it personally and couldn't see that I was attempting to teach them the responsibility that I had learned on my own, through experience. I paid rent and bills along with Marques and kept food in the house and as they began to make their money, I let them know that they were going to have to contribute more. They began to feel as if I was trying to take all their money, but it wasn't until later that they realized that all my money went to the house where they lived and everything else that they benefited from. Silas convinced Josiah that they could make it on their own and so after our little fall out, they took off. I found out later that they spent two weeks riding the Santa Monica bus line at night and slept on the beach until Mr. Nixon helped them get an apartment.

After paying rent and bills on their own, (apartment) they came back to apologize. When I think about it now, I must admit to myself that I was a little envious. Josiah had done so much more with so much less, in a shorter period. After all that I had done to that point and all the connections that I had made, I still was nowhere near where he was. It was like the time that Josiah brought me his first rhyme. He said, "take a look at this" and by the time I finished reading it, I realized that I had just read something special. I knew it was better than anything I had written to that point. (5 years of writing rhymes)

"Barcode analysis, we're powerless without wireless technology…not to me, but to GOD you owe apologies" (just a line from that rhyme)

As I have said, I don't live with regrets, but I am disappointed that I was not able to record my brother Josiah. I know he would have been a dope MC and it would have been a blessing to have his voice to hear anytime I wanted to be close to him. Since I do not, I must settle for his spirit. Pops had just got out of prison and came to live with me. And so, it turned out to be a Brocks reunion as Silas and Josiah had not seen their father in years. It was 4:30 AM on October 30, 1997, when I got the call from General Hospital. I remember Silas had spent the night. They said that Josiah had been shot and would not say where or if he was OK or not. They just said that we had to get down there. Pops, Silas, Marques, and I all jumped on the bus and headed there since we didn't have a car at the time. That was the quietest ten minutes of my life. It wasn't that far and when we got there, I'll never forget that little room they put us in. It felt like a padded room for a mental health facility, and I was going crazy. Not one of us said a word as we all had the same feeling I'm sure, it couldn't be good. The doctor finally got there, and he finally informed us after what felt like an infinite time frame that he had been shot in the head and he was officially diagnosed to be brain dead. I didn't really know what he meant or just didn't want to believe it as it was all a blank, my thoughts and emotions at that moment. Pops asked if we could see him and they took us into the room where he was and his body was still breathing as he was on "life support," but he was gone.

The whole thing was surreal. I didn't know how to react. I just remember blankness and seeing the same blank looks in the eyes of my brother Silas, Pops, and Marques. Silas spoke about some of his feelings for his brother, "As much as we fought, as much as we went through as brothers, that nigga was my heart." he said while crying. "We were so close; we were like nineteen months apart. We slept in the same bed together. He was my soul mate. He knew how I felt, and I knew how he felt. He would tell me shit about myself like you need to check yourself on this and you need to check yourself on that. It was just deep; we were just too tight. But we would fight like a mutha fucker, like cats and dogs," he breaks out into a laugh. "We had rules though. Nigga, we don't hit in the face. We gonna go body shots and if one of us slipped up and hit the other in the face, it was on, "oh, you hit me in the face?" Earlier that night, I asked him if he was sure he wanted to go with that cat "Cash." It was "Truly Odd" (a DJ who was there at the USC radio station that night) that he wanted to see, so I said alright."

I had known death at a young age, unfortunately from the man in the car in the alley to the time when Pops' older brother died of a drug overdose. (heroine) I was young, but I remember that night and when Pops got the call and when our doorbell got stuck for ten minutes as Pops felt that was his brother's spirit passing through, there were the "homies" (home boys/friends) from the hood, the ones we grew up with. ALL those "homies" from the hood. I lost count years ago and none of those hit as hard or as close to home as my baby bro.

Marques expressed himself on the matter, "Part of my heart was taken, he was ahead of his time and his age, he was an old soul," he said while he was choking up and starting to cry and show the raw emotion. "I was pissed! That wasn't supposed to happen to him, he was a good kid. He didn't bother nobody, and he died at the hands of what we fight against, it was a gang initiation. I really would like to sit down with those brothas and ask them what they were thinking, but I already know that they had already gave they souls to the devil. Hopefully for them, while they are where they at (prison) they will find our heavenly father Jesus Christ our

Lord and savior and get saved, even though they were doing the will of the devil, it hurts to this day, and I miss my lil dude."

I remember breaking down literally into a fetal position on the floor out in a hallway of the hospital and I remember having the most important people in my life with me, to support me. My little brother Silas was there, and Marques and Nik were there. Nik held me in her arms after I tried to smash the pain out of myself through my hands on the walls of the hospital. I've never felt a larger lump in my throat and hope I never again will. I couldn't breathe. I couldn't see but the blur, between the tears and the puff in my eyes. My body ached, and I wanted more than anything to not be there and to wake up from the nightmare. Those moments are forever for me, frozen in time in my mind burned and branded into my soul. Every now and then, I have to re-visit that to remind myself that I am still alive.

There were so many stories surrounding Josiah's death. The first of course was how it happened. Josiah and his promotional partner/associate/acquaintance "Cash" were with "Big Pun," short for "Punisher." He was a Hip-Hop artist they had picked him up from the Airport (LAX) earlier that day. He flew in from New York where he was from. They drove him around all day, to his "in-stores" (guest appearances at the record stores, for autograph signings and to promote their albums) and label executive meetings and radio interviews. They (Josiah and Cash) were leaving the final stop of which was the USC (University of Southern California) radio station. Cash was driving Josiah to his apartment in

Hollywood, and they were on the 101 Hollywood Freeway when it happened.

Josiah was half asleep in the passenger's seat and Cash said a car pulled up on his side, he said that the car was full and that he saw what he thought were Mexican "Cholos." (Latin gang members) He said they were "hitting him up" (flashing gang signs with hands and fingers) Cash said he sped off and away from them and that he told Josiah that they were "trippin'" (causing ruckus) Josiah must have been more concerned with his rest than the possibility of any sort of danger. Cash said they pulled up on his side again and this time he saw the gun. He said he tried to speed off again, and he ducked slightly as he did and that's when they shot, one single shot, went through the driver's window and through the driver's collar, according to him, it eventually made its way into the side of my little brother's head. His body was still breathing when Cash pulled off the freeway into a gas station, he called 911. When we got to the hospital, we had to make the decision to take him off life support since we knew he was brain dead, even though his body was still breathing. He was gone. We had to make the decision on whether to donate his organs. Josiah was only eighteen and in good health.

I remember waiting for my mother to make her way down from Seattle; she was indirectly blaming me for Josiah's death. Josiah made the decision to come down here with me and he decided to follow Silas to the Santa Monica bus line. Josiah made his own decisions, positive or negative, and up to that point, I would say that he had made mostly positive ones. I found out later from Moms that Josiah had a reoccurring nightmare about a red car chasing him. I also found out later from Rampart division detectives that were on Josiah's case, that it was a red Honda that the murderers were in. We also eventually found out from those same detectives, that they caught the culprits and that they all got life in prison. The ironic thing about that is that the Rampart division police department had a huge scandal involving some corrupt cops. I can say that they got this one right. Even more ironic is the fact that the lead detective in my brother's case, is married to a niece of my grandfather. I didn't find this out until my grandfather's funeral years later. He saw my mother's maiden name on the police report and recognized it as his wife's uncle's name, she was the one to tell my mother at the wake, the night before the funeral.

Josiah's murder was on the local news for the random freeway shooting angle as well as Josiah being somewhat known in the music industry. The hospital kept Josiah on life support until my mother and other family, were able to make it there to see him and say their goodbyes, after which they took his organs and we later found out that he had saved at least two lives. We received letters from the families. Josiah's remains were cremated as he had wished and eventually, we made our way back up to Seattle Washington to a "Vashon Island," where Josiah had spent some time. I had heard that when Josiah was still with Moms and her husband, he had run away to this island (a hippie colony) When we took the ferry over to this island, it was a gray day. We made our way to the shore where it was still gray, and the water was calm. When we released Jo's ashes into the water, a couple of minutes and a few individual thoughts later, (Moms, Silas, baby sisters Amber and Amanda and I) the water began to ripple and cause a few waves to crash to the shore. The sun peeked out for those few minutes and then it all went back to the way it was when we first arrived.

Josiah's "going home celebration" (funeral) (Christians say going home to be with the Lord, the bible says "to be absent from the body is to be present with the Lord") was like an industry/music event. There were record label executives, A&R's, producers, and artists. There were DJs and other underground artist and street promoters. It was held at our home church "Bible Enrichment International Fellowship Church." This is the church where I was baptized Christian, born again, where I became a member and received the "right hand of fellowship" and where I was later married. Since Josiah was cremated, there was a poster size picture of him posted just below the pulpit in the front of the church. Pastor Beverly "Bam" Crawford allowed us to run our own program, down to a play list. We had to get clean versions of all the songs. There was one song that we missed, it was by one of Josiah's favorite groups, "Boot Camp Click." The song was called, "No more trouble" and the line went something like; "My story doesn't know nothing about wining, I been losing like Mutha Fucker since the beginning." That curse word got by us, but our pastor cleaned it up for us pretty good. She said that even though she didn't condone the cursing, she understood it and said it was needed to emphasize the point.

$\mathcal{C}$HAPTER 16

(1997) *The so-called East vs. West Coast feud was escalated on March 9, when Notorious B.I.G. was shot and killed in a drive-by shooting after leaving a party for the Soul Train Music Awards in L.A. Notorious B.I.G.'s "Life After Death" album, days after his death, was released and became the best-selling hip-hop album of all time.*

Rapper Missy "Misdemeanor" Elliott released her acclaimed debut, "Supa Dupa Fly."

No Limit label owner Master P released "Ghetto D," inciting opportunities for New Orleans gangsta rappers

That has always been my feeling on certain things like "gang banging" and "dope slanging." (Drug dealing) I don't condone it, but I understand it. I don't condone genocide through violence or through enabling our peoples to kill themselves through drug abuse. But I understand why my peoples kill themselves; like dogs pit against each other in a confined space (cage). And, I understand why my peoples have and do sell drugs (as unfortunately I have) to survive.

This is done without regards to the effects it has on the peoples the drugs are being sold to. The excuse was, "if they don't buy it from me, they will buy it from someone."

I guess that's why when some of the homies from the hood said, "Let's ride for your brother!" This meant that they wanted me to go with them to find someone from the gang that killed my brother, and I was to pick one of them out and kill them as if this was to make up for one of them killing one of mine. I said, "Fuck that! It's not going to bring my brother back."

Another time God kept me away was the time that Marques was shot thirteen times, and I was across the street at the Barrigas.' The time when Marques and I were "frying" on acid (LSD) and Mixer came to the castle at the top of the hill. Mixer was coming to ask for Marques' gun, the chrome 380. He told us that the 18's (18th Street gang) had walked through the neighborhood with shotguns and that he was in a homeboy's Cadillac. He said that he was with a "heyna" (female) and he thought was the only reason that they didn't shoot him. So, instead of giving him the gun, Marques and I went with him down to Montclair to these abandoned apartments. Mixer and some of his "homeboys" went to "ride" (looked for the rival gang to shoot one or some of their members) on the 18's. I remember he said that they got one of them as they got back, and we hung out in the abandoned apartments and waited for them to come back.

Marques and I were still tripping on that acid, drinking and smoking weed as we had done many times before. The difference about this time was that while we were doing it, we were waiting for the "18's" to come back and retaliate for their loss. All we had was Marques' six shot 380 and there were at least ten of us down there. There was one Easy Rider who was drunk and as they the 18's rolled by he decided to jump out on the sidewalk and yell, "Fuck 18's!" It was dark in the abandoned apartment, and they couldn't see us, but we could see them across the street as they rolled up and parked. It was another one of Mixer's Easy Rider "homeboys" who told Marques to let them know we have something. Marques shot once and you could hear the bullet hit the steel gate in front of the apartment across the street. After that, all you could hear was bullets flying and hitting the abandoned apartment walls. We were all inside ducking down to avoid getting hit, while Marques hung out of the empty doorway conserving his ammunition but firing back. Sure enough, as we could hear every one of Marques' bullets hit that steel gate, one of them must have gotten close as their shots came to a halt. He did it, Marques held off what had to be two nine-millimeter caliber handguns, with his one trusty chrome six shot 380.

(Verse from Black & Brown Movement song "Young, Gifted and Brown")

"We need to stop all this violence that the young Blacks and Browns are facing,

Don't they know every ghetto is a Black and Brown nation?

You can't stop this non-profit, grew up with nothing but lint inside our pockets,

Identity crisis behind my eye sockets,

Black and Brown break down geologic,

Always caught between a rock and a hard place, first pair of name brands was Puma with the fat lace,

Young, gifted and brown with the white face, with the strength
to tear a mountain down at a snails' pace,
I remember when Chico was the man; I remember when it
was in to be Afro-Cuban,
I remember drum circles at Griffith Park with my old man,
I remember Moms stories about the "Civil Rights Movement."

My first son Juwan was born August 28, 1997, two months before Josiah died. Marques' second daughter/child Kahlah was born October 05, 1997, twenty-five days before Josiah died. He had the opportunity to meet them both and that was the last time I ever saw my brother. Kahlah was born at California Hospital, which is in downtown L.A. I remember the last conversation we had. We talked about the fact that he was able to see his father and talk with him and resolve some issues. The most important thing I remember about that time was the fact that this time was different. When in the past my little brother was trying to tell me something about myself, I wouldn't listen because I felt that he was my little brother and couldn't tell me nothing. This time God told me to listen, and I did, and I was blessed with his message. His last words to me were to keep doing the good I was doing, yet not to forget the things I must change and work on. He also said, "How can we call ourselves a Movement, if we are not moving." So, we keep moving.

(Excerpt from the Black and Brown Movement song "Brotha, I'm on your side")
"Brotha, I've been on your side since the beginning, whether
you were losing or wining, righteous or sinning. We communicated

just by grinning, knowing what's on the minds of each other.
Hermanos (brothers) by blood or not, we called ourselves brothers.
To my youngest, when you were born, I was 7 and when I was
25, you were 18 on your way to heaven. A.K.A., also known as
my brethren, we broke bread, we broke Levin; we were broke,
but knew where we were heading. And we remember where we
come from, from the African to the Aztec drum, from tequila
to Jamaican Rum, from the Black Panther Party to the Farm
Workers Union. Now days between Black and Brown, unity there
is none. There is racial conflict, riots, and violence. There are no
more African slaves and barely any Native Americans. What
happened to the pioneers like Pancho Sanchez and Miles Davis?
And we still don't see the similarities like the "Oldies" soul music
played in Latin "Low Riders."

My little brother Josiah Eljiah Brocks was murdered
and went home to be with his Father/God on October 30,
1997. The next day was Halloween and there was a show that
was set up by Bigga B and Orlando who were the two main
club promoters for "Unity." It was a traveling club that went
from Hollywood to downtown L.A. to the Inland Empire to
Orange County. It was really the theme of the club that stuck;
the idea that music, hip-hop (underground) and the specific
style of consciousness, that can bring about unity. Bigga B was
tight with Josiah as they worked together at "LOUD" records.
Bigga B was an A&R at Loud.

My cousins had come down from the Bay area and so
we rolled out to "Unity." This time it was downtown L.A.
and when we got there, using promotional stickers, a couple
of Jo's Street promo colleagues hit up RIP (Rest in Peace)

171

Josiah all over the club, inside and out. I'll never forget that lineup that night, "Common," "Most Def," "Taleb Kwalib" and I think "Twista." I got a chance to meet Most Def backstage before his performance. He gave me his condolences and told me about one of his peoples from New York who had fell victim to similar circumstances. He went on first that night and before his performance, him as well as all the other artists that night, all dedicated their sets to Josiah.

Bigga B later named his firstborn son after my little bro. He also had an artist by the name of "Xzibit" who gave a shout out (mentioned someone's name) to Josiah on the last song of his album "40 days and 40 nights" Close to a year later Bigga B was found dead in a hotel room somewhere out of town where he was on tour with one of his artists. Big Pun also passed away about a year after Josiah. There was an article that came out of "Details" magazine around that time and Big Pun was interviewed and quoted as saying that he felt responsible for Joe's death, since he had freestyled overtime that night, which caused Jo to leave late.

Like six degrees of separation, it seemed that we were always connected to the music and to the industry, LA Hip Hop in particular. Besides "Unity," there was "Elements," I mentioned previously. Marques' brother Joey was with us at club Elements one night and was battling at least 10 MC's that had stepped to him. He mowed them down one by one, but the promoters hated and wouldn't let him get on the stage to battle for money. There was Project Blowed as I mentioned previously, Marques went to Dorsey High School with Myka 9 (Freestyle Fellowship). Carlos Barriga and I performed at

Good Life Café. Later on, we would connect with other LA underground entities like Da Collective, Do it For Music, Radiotron (Carmelo), Universal Hip Hop Museum (West Coast), Delicious Vinyl/Pizza, Savages (Mic Hempstead), Hip Hop Caucus, Shneaky (MMup Clan). We connected with the craft beer scene that is directly connected with music, Socal Cerveceros (Ricky Ray Rivera / Coldchela), and Border X Brewery. We have continued our podcast on YouTube @ blackbrownmovement88, Black and Brown Movement Radio Podcast and 3rd Eye Worldwide Radio. We have hooked up with other podcasters like La Clika podcast and Recognition and Respect podcast.

As I stated previously there were a lot of sub-stories surrounding Josiah's life and death; the author who wrote that magazine article, also wrote a book featuring Jo's story, but more specifically was about one of Jo's closest friends Rah. (Rasheed) Rah was one of Josiah's Street promo partners, him, and Jo "rolled tuff," (went everywhere together) for a long time before their fallout. Rah was upset that Jo decided to leave their street promo crew that was called "Transit Crew." Jo went to join up with Cash and his crew, "Lock Down Promotions." I think "Kron Don" was part of their crew before he started his music and later acting career. There were rumors that Cash had a big mouth and that made me wonder if he had provoked those Cholos on the freeway. I don't know to this day, but I've always wondered if Rah was on to something?

After Jo was gone, things changed quite a bit. In the two years that he was a part of the music industry, he learned that he wasn't as interested in being a performer or in the forefront as he was being in the background and behind the scenes. I will never forget when I came home from Humboldt one of those school breaks, I was so excited to show Silas and Josiah the rhymes I had written and performed and what I was working on. I remember them shooting me back down to reality the way they always did in their own way. I think it was to let me know that I didn't have as much rhythm and flavor as them, but I was able to take their constructive criticism and use it to make my work better.

Josiah was working on a way to introduce us, the Black and Brown Movement, to the industry. He had this idea to put together a project that would involve some of the biggest and most prominent East Coast and West Coast artists. He called it the "Smash the Beef" project. In case you hadn't heard, there were some issues between West coast and East coast rappers/MC's, in the early to mid-nineties. It all came to a head with the murders of Tupac Shakur and Christopher Wallace ("Biggie Smalls.") The artists that Jo wanted to use for the project were all signed to the label that Jo worked mostly and closely with, Loud Records. The owners of Loud were the Rifkin's and I must thank them for their contributions to Josiah's going home celebration. Some of the artists including from the West coast: "Xzibit" and "The Alkaholics," from the East coast he wanted "Mob Deep" and "Fat Joe" and the "Wu-Tang Clan." There were other artists not on Loud Records that were also considered especially for their Black and Brown backgrounds. Cypress Hill was one of those groups, as well as

"KRS-ONE" who was like a lyrical mentor to Marques and me.

$\mathscr{C}$HAPTER 17

(1998) Puerto *Rican rapper Big Punisher released his debut,
"Capital Punishment," and was the first Hispanic MC with a
platinum album. Eminem's "The Slim Shady" was released on Dr.
Dre's Aftermath label and fast became a Billboard chart-topper.
Forbes magazine's "Top Moneymakers in Entertainment" list
included Russell Simmons, Master P and Puff Daddy. Puffy's
new clothing label and restaurant chain further cement his status
as a hip-hop mogul. White rock bands such as Korn and Limp
Bizkit combined rap with aggro rock and earned mainstream
radio success.*

Our Movement music began to take on a new life form
after Josiah had died. Our consciousness started to
reflect through the music and in areas other than the music
as well. In 1998, a year after Josiah's death, we the Movement
received an award from a woman's group called "Women in
Motion." It was the "Jericho" award and was presented to
the Black and Brown Movement for "Having the power and
strength within to tear down the walls of racial injustice for

racial harmony." We began to realize the power of our message whether it was through the music or through our actual movement. One of the most important things that Josiah said was, "we can't be a Movement if we are not moving." He meant out in the community and to this day, we have not and will not forget that. We had conceived the concept and had raised the ideals, but it was at this point that we began to feel the labor pains and the results were the birth of a Movement.

Civilization began in Africa and the "Black Panthers," "Brown Berets" and the death of Josiah Elijah Brocks both physically and metaphorically brought about the birth of the movement; physically in the forms of Juwan Antonio Lynn Brocks and Kahlah Ann Marie Jones, who are the nephew and niece born just before he passed. We always have and always will believe that "it takes a village to raise a child." The doctrine of our movement is rooted in our ancestral tribal government, from Africa to the seven tribes of Aztlan (southwestern area of the United States)

"Civilization began in Africa and through the migration; we arrived in Aztlan. From East to West, this makes us all peoples of the Sun. Through four hundred years of blood sweat and tears and through five hundred years of resistance, there are only a few things that we have sustained through bravery and persistence: the gospel, the culture and the music." (The anthem of the Movement)

From a spiritual aspect to a scientific aspect, all the signs point to Africa as the mother of civilization. The Bible talks about the Nile River in the book of Genesis. The first bones, human bones were found in Africa. The color scheme breaks down: black / brown / red / yellow / and white. You can get white from black, but you can't get black from white. I have done plenty of study and research regarding the subject.

(Verse from Black and Brown Movement song "Third Eye")

"One sky, one land and one time to shine, third eye. Now let me introduce the dynamics, starting out with pyramids bricks and artistically inscribed ceramics. This is an ethno-historical interpretation, from an indigenous "Mexica," to a Mestizo Xicano nation. Because of large scale immigration and due to an extremely high birth rate, my peoples now comprise the second largest ethno minority in the United States. Here in this land known to us as Aztlan, our authority is the majority of population won. Peoples of the Sun, pre-Columbian, Meso-American, all present before 30,000 BC (before Christ) and up to 1518 AD. (after the death of Christ) Our history will never be done once the Black and Brown culture of the sacred was born. We are the most important conceptual contribution to their social science. One sky, one land and one time to shine, third eye."

I remember in Humboldt when I was introduced to an older Native American gentleman who had an underground library. He told me that "it was the true history not his-story" and the "American library is where they bury the lies." I learned all about the similarities between Black and Brown and wondered why other peoples were caught up in all the differences and focused on only those differences. From East to West, from the rising of the Sun to the setting of the Sun, from tribe to tribe, from pyramid to pyramid; the similarities in religion, culture, and science to the similarities in music, the arts and communication. The similarities are undeniable.

Besides my mantra "balance is the key to life," my other would be, "take it to the source." This always meant for me that, whenever or wherever there was a problem or question or curiosity or a concern, I would take it the source for the answer. We all found out at an early age, individually, that we were leaders and not followers. We were always outside of the box, and we believe that it was God that brought us together. Our Movement is I.M.C. International and Multi-Cultural, which means, we have no borders, boundaries, limits, or gimmicks. We are worldwide.

After Josiah went home to be with the Lord, which happened in and around the times of the deaths of Tupac and Biggie; things regarding our music slowed down for a while. The connections to Josiah's life and death are numerous, just like Bigga B (A&R for Loud records back then) who named his firstborn son after Josiah. I named my second son after him as well and went ahead and gave him Jo's self-proclaimed middle name too, Elijah. The only reason my firstborn son didn't get the name was the fact that he was born almost exactly two months before Josiah passed away.

As we started to peace things back together and get back to our roots, our music, we began to realize the talent pool that existed in our own East L.A. area. I remember meeting Estephan Medina for the first time, it was in his garage/studio/hang out and it was Ricky (who was around at the time) who introduced us. Estephan is a musical genius, and

I found out firsthand that night in his garage. I guess it was a "jam session" (when musicians played together for fun and to fine tune their craft) Estephan's first weapon of choice is a guitar, which he plays masterfully. He reminds me of Carlos Santana. He can pretty much play any instrument and that night it was the drums, the bass, the keys (keyboard) and the flute. He was also the lead singer of and lead guitarist of a band he started; they went by the name of "Infinito." (infinite)

The Black and Brown Movement became friends of, brothers of, and musical/artistic partners of Estephan and Infinito. We supported them and they supported us. There were many jams/smoke sessions and many other musicians and artists that came through. Oh yeah, Estephan is an artist as well, sculptures, paintings, photography. As you might or might not know, along with genius, somehow and in some way comes with insanity. I say that to say that at times Estephan seemed to be a little scatter brained.

When we approached him to attempt to help promote his music and potentially get them a record deal, he wanted nothing to do with it. He saw the record industry to be evil. I had no problem with his perspective and even understood it. However, it was presented to him that there were several alternatives to going through the labels per say. Having the experience, I had obtained in the business side of the industry and knowing other ways to get his and their music out and to the point of making money, if not for any other reason than to allow them to continue to do what he and they loved to do and get paid to do it. To not have to worry about bills or making an income would be ideal to any artist, I would believe. But I guess not at the sacrifice of your art or beliefs. It was never about that for us, it was about doing it on our own like so many others have done successfully. When numerous efforts at persuasion failed, we requested that they at least play for us and at times they came to our home studio, individually. They played melodies, bass lines and drum beat behind, in and around our tracks. (music/songs)

(Verse from the Black and Brown Movement song "We taking over")

"We taking over, from here to Nova Scotia. While they slang that crack and "dozia" (weed/chronic) we slaingin boulders of knowledge, from the black asphalt streets to the white concrete stairs at your local college or university. Our adversity is to oversee the victory and triumph over Babylon at the heart of Zion is the heart of the lion of Judah. Can you see through them clouds of smoke of that Buddha? We ruder than dem rude boys, realer than dem real McCoy's. It's the Black and Brown B-Boys, here to bring the noise like P.E. Public Enemy # 1; yo it can't be done, like from the rising to the setting of the Sun. From Africa to Aztlan, it's the resurrection of the revolution."

One thing I can say for sure is that through the East L.A. connection and through the California State University of Los Angeles campus, we gained our affiliations and experiences and creative contributions to our masterpieces. Jerry was the drummer of "Infinito" and he brought this tall white boy with dreadlocks through to the garage. I think his name was Peter, and he was part of a band called "Burning Star." They were a reggae/hip-hip/rock fusion band. They had ties to the

181

"Black Eyed Peas." Jerry took us to "Black Eyed Peas" studio in Glendale California, where "Burning Star" rehearsed and recorded. Jerry brought to us one day, his idea of ITC. (Inner City Tribes)

I remember when I was a kid and dealing with identity crisis, I came to my father (Pops/De Franco Brocks) with the issue and told him that they were calling me a mutt (a dog mixed with many breeds) at school. I didn't understand as I knew I wasn't a dog, Pops told me to tell them that I am IMC (International Multi-Cultural)

Then there was Bruce Roberts who moved in across the street from us at Lafler Road, when we lived up from Cal State L.A. It was Vince Wong (I will get to him in a bit) who introduced us to Bruce. I think he heard music coming from our house and introduced himself to Vince. We came home one day, and Bruce was in the studio with Vince, working on a song. Bruce is originally from New York and made his way out West to go to school and pursue his musical aspirations. He also is an extremely talented individual and had worked with and had ties to some established artists on both the East and West coasts. He had also worked in the movie industry as that was one of his passions as well. Bruce introduced us to a lot of aspiring artists who came and went, but a lot of times when they came, they brought with them resources.

Some of those resources came in the form of Lance who had a passion for writing and had such a delivery and smooth voice. The problem for him was the fact that he wasn't local and that his father was extremely strict and of course he lived with his parents. Then there was David who went to school for film and wanted to rhyme but was still rather raw. He ended up taking the copies of songs that we gave him, that he was on was selling them without our permission. We got through that later. There was KiKi who spit/flowed in Spanish and represented the Latin perspective and the Movement. KiKi, aka "Next," has always been and will always be an honorary member of the Movement.

Marques met other Brown members Jess and Davey D via East LA College. We worked with Davey D for a while since he had a home studio in the back of his parent's house and eventually a loft studio in downtown LA. He gave us tracks he had made with his partner Fish and on his own. We also did a show with Davey D at Hollywood's "Knitting Factory." Talented artists came and went. Every member, no matter how short lived their membership, was important if they contributed something that left a mark.

There was also a Brown female representation via rhyming and singing. The music and the vibe brought a lot of characters/artists through 2205 Lafler Road and one of them was Vince who was a Chinese dude with dreadlocks and was also a musician.

He played guitar, and he needed a place to stay. After discussing it, Marques and I decided to give it a try. Vince ended up building a loft in the master bedroom and turned the rest of the room into a recording studio. Vince used the money that he made recording, mostly musicians, to pay his portion of rent and bills. And, for the first few months there were no problems. One time I will never forget, he recorded a ten-piece band named, "Quinto Sol." They were local to East

L.A. Most of them fit into the studio, except for the bass that got put in the bathroom and a couple of horns that were in the living room. There were other smaller bands and other solo musicians that he recorded. We even recorded a couple of songs with him.

There were other musicians that we met through Vince, and we ended up putting a band together of our own. Vince was lead guitarist and to be honest there were so many that came and went, for the life of me I couldn't tell you all their names. There was a "Rhodes" keyboard, bass, drums, and percussions. (congas & bongos) There were some cool "katz" and they took me back to my origins in Humboldt and it was a lot of fun. Oh yeah, we were the vocalist/MCs. I would imagine the reason I don't remember their names was since we only lasted as a band for about four rehearsals and two shows. Both shows were held at the "Old Town Pub," in Old Town Monrovia.

I'll never forget those shows, for the shows that we put on. The first show we started with a "soul clap" and when it looked like the crowd wasn't into it, we all jumped off the stage and into the crowd and got them into it. The second show started with us being introduced but not being on the stage… we were dispersed among the crowd and at the bar… the announcer asked if there were any musicians in the crowd, the band then made their way to the stage and began tuning up their instruments. The announcer left the stage and Vince jumped on the Mic (microphone) and asked if there were any MCs in the crowd. There were five of us that night and we came from all angles, the band was tuned up and we rocked it!

The first sign of danger came that night, after that show. Towards the end of our set, he stood up from his "Rhodes" keyboard (I don't know if he ever really knew what he had in that keyboard) and interrupted the last song of the set to go into some other song that we had not rehearsed. Come to find out later that he was a "Coke (cocaine) head" and an alcoholic. The problem was that he had to indulge before a show to go on, this was always a risk considering that his behavior during the show could be unpredictable. Shortly after our short-lived band experience dissipated, so did the roommate situation with Vince.

He began to struggle for about a month and a half and didn't pay his full portion of rent and bills. He then told us that he was going to go home to China for a month and when he came back, he would pay us what he owed, plus some. We knew something was up as we thought how he was in debt with us, and he wasn't booking any recording sessions. The question was how was he able to come up with the funds to go to China? And why he just didn't pay us with those funds? He said he had something going on back home and would be able to come back with enough to pay us and set himself up for a while.

While he was gone, we heard a few different stories about his trip, his plans and about him from a few of his associates. We heard that he was having financial issues due to a drug problem and that he got the money to go from his parents who wanted him to get away from the "states" (United States) and that environment. We heard that it was a trip for fun and that when he got back, he didn't plan on paying us and planned on moving out. While he was gone, we took the liberty of securing a couple of pieces of his studio; seeing that we noticed that some of the bigger pieces were gone before he left. When he came back, within that same week, he waited until we were gone and when we came back, the studio and the room were cleaned out. He wouldn't answer his phone and shortly after that we were served some papers from small claims court. Before the court day, he came to the house with the police who told us that we couldn't hold his equipment for the money he owed us. So, we gave it back and when we went to court, we settled the whole situation.

After getting over that mess, we again got back to work, recording our catalog, and doing a few shows locally. MCs came and went, bringing with them producers and tracks (songs) and talent. Around this time is when Bruce, brought JAH (Jerry) around the Movement. JAH had a natural energy that was positive and uplifting. He was young and vibrant and charismatic. He was a "dread," (Dreadlock Rastafarian) listened to Reggae music, ate healthy and chewed "ginger root." (A root found in the Caribbean and chewed for its flavor as well as its ability to clean and strengthen teeth) Most of all JAH (Jerry) was talented. He played electric bass and I'm not sure what other instruments he might have played. One thing I do know was that Jerry had rhymes.

("JAH" Jerry's verse from the Black and Brown Movement song "Ghetto Winds")

"How do you think you can defeat me with your 3rd string QB (Quarter Back) B&B (Black and Brown) can run back 100-yard kickoff returns easily. I'll take it back to '93', socks over my cleats. Clothesline pork rinds...Fuck a 5-yard penalty; it's all about the

*fun of the game. No rules in the streets; it's the Gods vs. the pigs.
The new expansion teams are in a battle for ghetto territory. We
are not playing for rings; we smoke super bowls and cut pig skins
deep. We are in the red zone, suckas head home. They know we
head strong, while they are dead wrong. My 3rd eye formation's
penetrating the pig's goal line "D." That's why you'll find me in the
e-n-d-z-o-n-e on 3 downs. And it maddens me when brothers
who are locked down and free men don't recognize the enemy.
B&B will rise to the top with vision and mental mastery. It was
a 1st quarter blow out, pigs 0 and Gods 63."*

JAH started coming around more often and almost
immediately took to the Movement as we took to him. We
used his bass skills on a couple of tracks and gave him a few
verses on a few other songs. We eternally infused our bond
when we recorded professionally at a studio just outside of
Hollywood in Studio City. We did a show in West Covina
at a venue called the "Dogg House." That night there were a
couple of acts before us, and we got there early. There were six
of us; six MC's performing off a prerecorded CD (compact
disc) with tracks. So, by arriving to the show early, you would
think we might have had an advantage of being more prepared
for a better performance. There was a bar, and we had not yet
implemented our two-drink minimum before a show rule.

Just before the first act came on stage, there was a DJ (disk
jockey /someone who plays music through either a record
on a turntable or CDs) who was playing some old school
B-Boy cuts. (B-Boy = Hip-Hop = Graffiti = Break dancing =
Rhyming and DJing) Bruce, our eldest member, was feeling
his oats that night, of course this only after a few drinks.
He decided he was going to get in touch with his roots and

busted out a "break dance" routine. The thing that none of us expected was that Bruce's break dancing would lead to an ankle breaking. It did just that as well as causing Bruce to vomit in his beanie since he couldn't make it to the restroom. He ended up doing the show on one leg; then he went to the hospital.

The show went well otherwise and after the show, was the next chapter, on our way to the car we ran into a "freestyle session," we later found out that we were rhyming with a local group that we had heard of and that later played a part in the Movement's story. They were called "The Missing Page Crew." We ended up hooking up with one of their members at East Los Angeles Community College, where both Marques and I attended. ELAC was another hotbed of talent.

His name was Vernon, we called him "Vern." He was like so many that had come before him and after him. They all had talent, some more than others, they all felt the vibe that we give off as they came in and out of the circle. The problem always seemed to be that every MC/artist that came through our doors, no matter how many times, they always had prior affiliations and associations that prevented them from fully committing to the Black and Brown Movement. There has always been that gorilla on our back and that elephant in the room that is known as survival. It has always been the determining factor in the productivity and overall success of us. Some if not most of our younger artistic partners, who of course didn't have the same responsibilities as Marques and me, just could not understand that. They lived at home with their parents and didn't have kids like we did. They might have had jobs or went to school, but other than that their only real responsibility was themselves.

$\mathscr{C}$ HAPTER 18

(1999) *Ex-Fugees member Lauryn Hill released her first solo album, "The Miseducation of Lauryn Hill," it won five Grammy awards.*

Black Star, featuring Talib Kweli and Mos Def, released its debut album, making a way for a resurgence of conscious lyrics and alternative rap.

Southern-based record labels such as Cash Money Records and artists including Ludacris, Juvenile, Lil Wayne and the Hypnotized Mindz Camp signaled the rise of the Dirty South's reign in hip-hop.

Puff Daddy and his then girlfriend Jennifer Lopez tussled with patrons at a New Year's Eve club party. When the shooting ensued, they fled the scene and were later arrested for aggravated assault.)

The one youngster I always felt the most was JAH (Jerry). He was humble and always understood when survival took precedence to the music. He was attending Cal State Dominguez Hills and lived on the campus. He had a job and was involved in some community activities; we were not prepared for what happened next. We got the call early in the afternoon from Bruce, who brought JAH to the cipher. He was found in his dorm room early that morning. He had passed away at the age of twenty-one. It was heart failure, but he was a health nut? Come to find out that his father had died at an early age of the same thing. It was baffling and was happening again and another "Young Prophet" had left us. We knew he went home to be with his father. (God/biological) We knew he was in a better place along with our brother Josiah.

(Verse from the Black and Brown Movement song "My Peoples, My Peoples")

"The Sun, the Moon and the Stars…the omnipresent one will soon spars with the devil on his level. He is the creator, the animator and the originator of life and death. This is for my peeps, keep it close to, it's what we're supposed to do, but what most do is fall victim to the trends and the fashions. We keep our feet to the concrete and keep mashing. You are a slave to society, in it for the name, the fame and notoriety. You're like a summer breeze and you think you feel fine, blowing all the brain cells in your mind. My peoples, my peoples, you should be happy and don't worry. You could be gone tomorrow, dead and buried. No pain, no torture, no sorrow, who did you follow and who did you lead, did you plant your seed? Tell me did you ever read the book? Did you ever take a look at the bigger picture? I know you bled, but no longer will you bleed…we will never be equal, but you'll always be my peoples. My peoples, my peoples, we gots to give love to…My peoples, my peoples are the Black and Brown Movement…we put nothing

above, our peoples, our peoples, we are tired of losing our peoples."

We attended Jerry's going home services (funeral) as a Movement and in solidarity we presented his family with a CD of the work he had done with us. We also gave his family the necklace with charm that we passed around the MC crew, who ever came up with the hottest rhyme on a song got to wear it until someone came with a hotter verse. He was so tight that when he passed, we decided to retire it. So, again we had to adjust and had to move on. We had to stay the course for those who had gone and for those who were still here. Being as spiritual as we are, not as religious and there is a difference, faith has always kept us on one accord. The path of faith is grounded in our personal relationships with God. See that thing about religion is that it is a "man-made" concept and if a man is not perfect, then religion is not perfect. The only thing that is perfect other than God is spirituality in its essence.

It wasn't until Humboldt (college) when I took my first college course related to religion. That's when I realized, there are so many more religions that I ever knew about. I figured I could make my own educated decision. I remember gravitating towards Christianity and Islam and Rastafarianism. There were aspects of each religion that I agree with, believed in, and thought that I was going to transport to my own "created" religion. Until I realized that might be mistaken for a cult.

When Marques and I decided to get out of the drug trafficking game, it was God's call that we answered and that's when we knew it was time to strengthen our personal relationships with him. We visited a couple of Christian churches with our friend Avery from the neighborhood, who attended UCLA (University of California Los Angeles) Unfortunately our first experience didn't draw us in, instead it pushed us farther away. We later evaluated the situation and realized that the heavy, Old Testament laden church that we first visited, was laced with sexist tendencies. I realize that is a deep and flammable statement, so let me break it down. The Old Testament, which is basically the first half of the Bible, is geared towards male dominance. Women were to take a back seat in every sense of the word and to the extreme. In turn, this only promoted intense male bonding/fellowship which was uncomfortable and didn't work for us.

We had too much love and respect for the woman in our lives. We didn't/don't always agree with them and had/have our issues with them as they had/have their personal problems. Both Marques and I were raised mostly by the women in our families, considering the absence of our fathers or any other male figures/role models. We ended up going back to a church we were familiar with, a church we had been to and has a female pastor. Bible Enrichment Fellowship International Church (BEFIC) is in

Inglewood California: the presiding pastor, Apostle is Beverly "Bam" Crawford. She is

Known as "Bam" for the way she delivers God's word/ good news. It's a small world we live in and in Los Angeles/ Hollywood as spread out as it is, graphically, it is just as small. From the Christian world to the entertainment industry, to the work force, it always seems like everybody knows everybody in these circles. Pastor "Bam" came from one of the biggest Christian churches in Los Angeles, Crenshaw Christian Center. My second Moms (Connie, Marques' mother) first attended her services, and she followed when pastor started BEFIC (the home church of the Black and Brown Movement)

Over the years that we have been associated with and members of Bible Enrichment, we attempted to work with them on a Movement level, be it spiritual, musical, or social. We have on smaller levels but have not yet been involved enough with the church and have always had the "survival factor." (As a crutch) As we have gotten older though, we have seen the errors in our ways and have seen the need to get more involved on many levels.

As I mentioned previously, it goes back to what Josiah said before he passed, "How can we be a Movement, if we're not moving?" So, we moved as much as we could within our world/realm. We reached out to other "grassroots" organizations; we spread our message through poetry readings and through our music performed at smaller venues and music played on local radio stations. One of those radio stations was KPFK 90.7 FM out of Los Angeles to Santa Barbara; this is a non-profit radio station, public access.

We always did and have done what we could to network with those who have similar interests. We met Mike Skilo and joined "In the Cutt Productions." Mike is a producer, and an engineer that we signed a 50-50 split contract with some years ago. We recorded songs with him, that he either produced or engineered. We helped him film and edit a couple of music videos he produced and co-directed. The videos were for other artists he produced and engineered for. We have made some meaningful music with Mike over the years.

We have always spread the word/message, where and when we could. Whether it was our very first performance, (Carlos and I) at the "Good Life Café" on Crenshaw Boulevard, or whether it was one of the last shows we did at the "Knitting Factory" in Hollywood. Whether it was the house parties and underground Hip-Hop shows and MC battles and various clubs or hot spots, we always represented the Movement. There have been a few times where in certain situations, like the time I was at a house party in South Central Los Angeles, there were a few Mexican gang members who approached me after I came off the microphone. They questioned me regarding the Black portion of the Black & Brown Movement, "Why does the Black have to be first?" I explained it to them, but they just did not want to get it. They wanted to dispute the facts and wanted to FIGHT the TRUTH as they have fought Black folks most of their lives, (that's all they have ever known) on some level or another. We always knew that we would be met with some resistance as what we created, was not of the popular line of thought. (Especially where we grew up)

Once Carlos (Barriga) had stepped down as "Founding Father," Marques stepped up and our first performance was a showcase at Hollywood's infamous "Comedy Store." Marques explained the feeling he got when he first performed, "Jacked, juiced, it was exhilarating to be able to speak and say eloquent things that could touch people and enlighten them. What gets me excited is that I am giving out positive testimony and a testament to my life and what I represent. It was like a crack addict on his first hit, sparked.' Before we went on that night, we had a few of our people backstage with us. One of the homies was having issues backstage, I think it was "baby mama" drama, I didn't see it, but they said she was in his face, and he laid her out and broke out of the backdoor. This was the first time we had incorporated acting in a musical stage performance. Marques and I came up with a skit that had him at one end of the stage, and I was on the other, with Money K sitting on a stool in the middle of the stage (center stage) The skit consisted of Marques and I rushing at each other from opposite sides of the stage, we yelled racial slurs at each other while pushing on each other. Our Movement brother Money K (vocalist/singer) who was sitting on a stool (center stage) jumped up and separated us and said, "Why are you fighting with each other? Don't you know that you are Black and Brown?"

CHAPTER 19

From this point going forward you will notice that I will abandon the hip-hop timeline within the story, since for me, that is when the best hip-hop of all time existed. From 2000 to 2010 and 2010 to 2020, don't get me wrong, there was some good music. There are some MC's that need to be mentioned in that timeline, like Kendrick Lamar, Nipsy Hustle, J Cole, Eminem, Mos Def, Talib Kweli, Chance the Rapper, and Nas. KRS ONE has always been timeless and in 1999 during the transition to the new millennium, I was blessed to have been interviewed by him. Marques was supposed to do the interview but gave it to me and even though we are of the same entity, I will be forever grateful. KRS asked me, "what should Hip Hop be doing in the new millennium?" I replied, "Hip Hop should be going into the community more, kind of like the athletes do in terms of the charities and working with the churches and schools and the youth, like you do. Start going to the colleges and speak to these people and educate them more about Hip Hop and what they do. Show more examples, not necessarily role models but good examples, in terms of contributing to the community where their making their money from."

They kept me loving Hip Hop during that time. This is only my opinion and like they say about opinions, everyone has one, like they have an asshole. I have been called and known to be at times, one of those.

Wherever we were and whatever we did, we always represented the Movement and its ideals. These ideals are what the Movement is built upon, like that of the "Civil Rights Movement," the "Black Panthers" and the "Chicano Movement" which included the "Brown Berets/Brown Pride" and "La Raza." (The race) We as well incorporated many of the same beliefs and doctrine. We followed the leads set forth by Martin Luther King Jr., Malcolm X, Marcus Garvey, Bob Marley, Pancho Villa, Miguel Hidalgo, Che Gueverra, Cesar Chavez and John F. Kennedy. From Montgomery Alabama to Harlem to Mecca to Africa to Jamaica to Mexico to South America, these men's universal messages of freedom, justice, equality, pride, integrity, and brotherhood spanned the globe. From our studies in history, sociology, psychology, language, culture, art, music, religion, and science, we gathered our influences like ingredients to a recipe. History, from the beginning of civilization to the African slave trade to the historical era of this nation's first Black president, (Barack Obama) has taken numerous shapes. Sociology as the study of societies has taught us the makeup of our community and compared it to others in its organization and lack thereof. Psychology showed us to examine our minds and evaluate the functionality of them as related to our behaviors. Language revealed to us the need, purpose, and value of communication through verbal and nonverbal expression.

We learned through our living experiences, traditions and practices about our own cultures, subcultures, and blended cultures. Art from its inception in drawings on cave walls to graffiti on neighborhood brick walls, it has always been present. Our musical influences range from African and Latin rhythms to world beat to Reggae to Jazz to Funk to R&B and Hip-Hop. We studied music from theory to reading, writing, and playing instruments to vocals.

Religion can be first found in Neanderthal burial rituals, like modern day funerals. Religion can be considered the cornerstone and foundational to all societies and cultures. Yet, it is spirituality that guides us and leads us to our moral compass. We always used our knowledge of science as proving grounds to what we believe in. Civilization began in Africa and science helped us to prove that. Pain, conflict, poverty, desperation, and despair all contribute to the makeup of the downtrodden. When you don't have anything, it makes it easier not to care about anything. When all you see is the worst this world has to offer, hope becomes a thing in dreams and fantasies if at all. Hunger causes a negative chain reaction that includes anger and rage and a lack of energy.

It's the quietest storm we are to worry about. When things build inside, they can erupt like a volcano, after festering for so long. It is much easier to deal with a reality that exists directly in front of us. I know much more about and can relate more to the "rags" then I do and can to the "riches" of the world. Most of this globe would fall into that category/ status of "third world". The criteria to that is poverty, lack of clean water or food and minimal to no healthcare. These disease-stricken lands of our earth represent too many of our world neighbors.

$\mathcal{C}$HAPTER 20

I remember my mother being a recipient of County "welfare" benefits; but growing up I really couldn't recognize the benefit or assistance. I remember having to eat beans and rice for months straight, not to complain as of course there were/ are those of our own world's citizens in the same situation as well as those who had/have nothing to eat at all. I also knew growing up that we were well below America's "poverty level." We were poor, but Moms did her best to make sure we had at least the basics. We had a roof over our heads, we had food to eat, (whatever it was) and we had clothes and shoes to wear.

The clothes and shoes were usually not the name brands, which I probably wouldn't have cared about, had it not been for the mean kids at school. How many of you can relate with the "mean" kids at school? And does it matter the grade or level? The biggest problem was the kids whose parents had a little bit of money and were at a level between poor to middle class. These kids had most of the name brands and would harass you if you didn't. They would then "click up" (get together) with their own kind, which then got you harassed by a group. Who remembers the "bagging,' the "capping?" For those who didn't have it, we did have pride and integrity and of course our fists. So, fights were inevitable.

I remember when my eldest cousin stayed with us one summer, after returning from the Marines Corps boot camp. He showed me some moves he had learned. He had some weapons he had imported as well. Some of his moves were basic hand to hand combat inspired, others were Judo and Jujitsu inspired. (Martial arts) The weapons included nun –chucks and butterfly knives. A couple of moves that he showed me were a counterpunch toss, when someone threw a punch at you, you would grab them by their wrists with one hand and lock their elbow with the other. You would then use the momentum they built by lunging at you, to toss them. The other move was a close combat move where with one hand you would grab the enemy by their chin and with the other hand you grab the back of their head. You would then, with force and not speed, twist their head until their body followed. If you didn't do it right, you could break their neck.

He also showed me how to use the butterfly knives. So, when I was in junior high and was having an issue with a bully, I called upon what my cousin had showed me. I knew I couldn't use the knife or knives without a bad ending. When he tried to punch me, I performed the first move and when he approached me again, I used the second move. Now the second move made me nervous, but I was able to do it right and by the time it was over, I was standing over the bully with him on his back and his head in my hands. I would've paid anything for a picture of the reaction on his face.

Who remembers Pro Wings, Pro Keds or Bubble Gums? (Cheap, generic brand sneakers) Who can relate with Tough

Skins Wranglers or Cowboys? (Jeans) I just wanted some Levi's 501's and some Nikes or Adidas or Reeboks or Pumas. Imagine how excited I was when I got my first pair of Levi's 501's and Pony basketball shoes. I was cool with the Pony's, they weren't the top of the line, but they were name brand and would keep me from getting teased. It's always been about the name brands vs. generic and has always been about the haves vs. the have nots.

(This was found on a post-it and was written in a moment of financial frustration)

"I'm broke! The hands of poverty have got me in a choke hold! Gots to be bold, but it's hard without silver or gold. I've never had enough green, how many of you know what I mean? Without enough money, thing's just don't seem that funny. I read that book, "Get rich quick for Dummies." Without money, most days just don't seem that sunny. Most days seem cloudy…I say it loudly… broke starts with a B and ends with E. Now that I found him, my days start with a "hap" and end with a "py." Money can't do nothing for me but keep me worldly debt free. I can never repay the debt to Jesus for giving his life for me on Calvary. If I have stock and commodity in my G-O-D, I can never be B-R-O-K-E."

$\mathcal{C}$HAPTER 21

I have always taken pride in being reliable. Those closest to me always knew they could depend on me. Whether it was financially (Now keep in mind, for most of my life, I have not had lots of money) knowing if I had it and they needed, they could get it. Or they knew I would go and figure out how to get it. Whether it was emotionally, physically, or mentally; they knew that they could lean on me, at times. I always knew that if I wasn't there, somehow and some way it would get done. I guess I got used to this at an early age and it became part of my identity. I suppose I became dependent on being dependable since there was such a lack of dependability in my childhood. It felt good to be able to come through for those closest to me. I later realized that this was a crutch for me and at times it was to the detriment of myself. I had to recognize this and make sure that I was also taking care of myself, remember, balance is the key to life. Day and night, light and dark, the Sun and Moon, fire, and water. It is the duality of the universe.

This leads me to the point of mental/behavioral stability. I have mentioned "survival mode," I have mentioned excuses, I have mentioned crutches, and I have not mentioned therapy.

If you are from the hood, you should be aware of the stigmas associated with that word. Unfortunately, most of our Black and Brown people don't believe in it. The excuse, "I'm not going to talk to someone I don't know and who doesn't know me." The crutch, "I'm not going to talk about my feelings, that's for white people." The reasoning, "I'm not going to pay someone to talk to them." When I talk about survival mode, I am referring to seeing or hearing things that you know are or were wrong and instead of dealing with them, you forget them and move on. You do not actually forget them; you push them deep down outside. If you try to run from your issues, they just follow you. I have always been a problem solver, if there is a problem, let's find a solution. This can also refer to other people's problems. I have tended to take on the problems of those I love. It is time for me to take therapy head on, like a problem that needs to be solved. It is time to unpack the boxes. My behavior that has not dealt with things, has affected my relationships, my psyche, my emotional intelligence, and my life. Marques has dealt with mental health issues; Ricky has dealt with mental health issues. Many of our family members have dealt with mental health issues. Drugs and alcohol are used to mask the truth within. It is OK to talk to someone you don't know. It is all about perspective. If you look at it, they do not know you either. They are objective and do not have preconceived notions, they have a job to do. If they do not care about you, because they do not know, I'm sure most of them care about their jobs and doing a good job of helping their patients.

I have known and/or figured out that around the age of twelve is when I really got in tune with my inner "asshole."

I'll never forget the day my mother and I had just gotten back from the laundromat. We had walked because we didn't have a car at the time, using a shopping cart from the grocery store, it was a good distance too. So, we finally got home, and I was on the living room floor, folding clothes. I don't remember what I said, but I know it was a smart-ass remark. I used to say it was better to be a smart-ass than a dumb one. She snapped on me, which she rarely had done, and she started beating on my back while I was bent over still folding clothes. I remember standing up while she was still hitting me, and I asked her, "are you done?" She really went off then, again, which she had rarely done.

I know that I am not the easiest person to get along with. I know that for years; I had a problem with communication and expressing myself. There was not a lot of communication in my household while growing up. There wasn't a lot of communication in my mother's household. There was no question that Moms loved us but there just wasn't a lot of affection going around. There wasn't a lot of affection given to my mother. These continued behaviors continued the vicious cycles. I learned to attempt to understand. I don't have to condone certain behaviors and actions, yet if I attempt to understand them, I can learn where they come from. I have done my best not to repeat the cycles, to the point of overcompensation. I didn't beat my children because I was beaten as a child. I have been thrown up against a wall and sat on a hot stove. I was afraid if I spanked my children too much, I would fall into the trap of losing control and taking out my issues on my kids. That is what I felt was done to me. At times I have come to regret that decision when my children have gotten a bit too mouthy or out of control. Overall, I have helped to raise great kids and now young adults.

$\mathscr{C}$HAPTER 22

As I grew old enough to understand, I again had to take it to the source to figure out why all that was? Knowing the story of my family tree and more specifically about how my mom grew up, I began to piece it together and realize that Moms being in the middle of ten siblings, must have lacked affection as well. I remember Moms telling me about how she grew up and how her mother was always gone, out and about and how she partied with no regards to consequence. Moms said she got out every chance she could as she lived in the Bay Area for most of her childhood and teen years, at that time it was all about sex, drugs and rock and roll. They lived in the "Mission District" of San Francisco during mom's high school years, and she went to Mission high school. This is where she met Pops when she was fifteen, she said they dated and when she was sixteen, she was introduced by her lifelong friend to my biological father. He was a little older than them, it took me until just recently to find out he was manipulative, a liar, and a child molester. I found out partially from Moms, only after learning from my newly found brother.

The only thing I knew about my biological father was his name. Daniel Williamson.

When I received the message on my "My Space" (I know that is a long time ago in social media years) page that said it was from a brother I never met, I was shocked. I was up in the Bay Area visiting my little brother Silas and his family when I saw the message. My newfound brother Jason left his cell phone number which had a Bay area code, so I knew he was up there as well. I was on a four-day weekend and left that Monday, which was Martin Luther King Jr. day. I was able to meet him that day just before I left. I met him, his girlfriend at the time (who is now his wife) and his only child/daughter/my niece who is the same age as my son Juwan. He got to meet Pops and my little brother Silas and his sons and my sons.

The first thing he said to me was that I did not miss anything regarding not having him around as a father. My new younger brother Jason is the same age as my brother Silas. I also have another brother who is six months younger than me. That means I am still the oldest. Jason told me that our father used to sit in with (play music with, but not a part of a band) "Sly and the Family Stone," a funk band from the 1970s. Jason said that he played guitar and bass. My Mom said that when I was very young, my biological father tried to see me, but she did not feel comfortable with that and I'm glad she didn't. I am just now old to see where my musical talents come from and now, I know for sure my racial makeup. Mostly Mexican, Cherokee Indian, Norwegian, Irish, and Scottish. I have learned so much about myself in the recent and over my life span. I have learned so much about my history and in general.

Some years back my grandmother Elizabeth Gillis-Montemayor (a.k.a. Granny Mom) had a major stroke. Those years back I was down in San Diego where she lived, it turned into one of those forced family reunions. (Emergencies, funerals, weddings, births) It was an opportunity to catch up with family I hadn't seen in a while as well as a chance to reminisce. More importantly, I learned some more family history that was extremely dark, but gave insight into how things developed with my family. It was one of my aunties who dropped the "bomb" on me.

She started with a background on my great-grandmother; we called her "Abuelita," which is Spanish for grandmother. She was born in the year 1900 and died in the year 1992. In the early nineteen-hundreds, her family worked for the royal family of Mexico, as seamstresses. She married at sixteen; he was a Scotch/Irish Captain in the Navy. (My great-grandfather) They moved to the states (US) and had two children, my grandmother, and her brother Steve. They eventually moved back to Mexico and started a couple of small businesses and began to buy up some properties in the Tijuana area of Mexico. With the combination of my great-grandpa's military income and the businesses and the properties, especially at that time, they were probably considered well off.

With their financial status, it afforded my great-grandmother the luxury of assistance by the way of maids. And as my grandmother grew up, it was the maids that raised her. At an early age, with her parents mostly gone all the time, she began to become rebellious. Come to find out, she started drinking at age fourteen and she became an alcoholic. It all came to a head when she was raped, still at the age fourteen. That said a lot for where my family is today. It also said a lot for her eleven children, and the almost same amount of fathers/sperm donors.

CHAPTER 23

Ido not know much about my grandfather as I said before. I have only met him a few times in my life. There are more women/females in our family than men. And the men in our family have had their issues, whether it was due to having more females in their lives or the fact of not having their fathers around or any other male figures/role models. I have had some of the same issues. There was a lack of a male presence, let alone fatherhood, leadership, or any sort of a positive example. Instead, what I saw growing up, was a lot of leaving and giving up and giving into addictions, whether they were bad behavior, alcohol or drug related.

It seems to be hereditary, from generation to generation, continuously falling into the same traps. Whether it was the Willie Lynch letters, or the Native American holocaust. Whether it the demise of the Black Panthers and the Brown Berets. The fall of Dr. King and Malcom X, the death of the Civil Rights Movement (some may argue it's not dead). It could be the policing/military state, the systematic racism, or the system itself, that was never made for us, just from us. Institutionalization, poverty with no economic resources, and no access to quality education, all contribute to the cursing of our people. The only way that a "New World Order" can succeed is when the majority/masses of society are broken and not able to resist on the levels that matter. When you cut the head of the family, that family will suffer and tend to be dysfunctional and that is the curse that has continued throughout the generations.

As the men fell to the wayside, the women had to overcompensate to try to fill the void. This is how "angry women syndrome" was born. One of my theories is that the reason men started losing their value was due to those boys/males, which stopped seeing the responsibility of being a man. It is an honor to be a man, but along with that honor comes responsibility and those boys/males that do not see it as an honor, will not see a responsibility to live up to.

The majority of my uncle's, other than my uncle Johnny who graduated from UCLA at age thirty, had major issues. Their issues ranged from drugs and alcohol to mental and emotional instability. My older cousins also did their best with what they had, but sometimes too busy surviving and living to develop further. Some of them followed their father's footsteps, good or bad. I am not the one to judge them or any other mortal for that matter, that is for God to do. I do not have to like what I see and can want more for my people. They must want more for themselves unless they are content. If they like it, I love it. I will do my best to understand. Most of what I have learned about being a man has been learned on my own and through my own life experiences. From what I know, there is no handbook or instructions… no wait, there is the BIBLE.

Basic - Instructions - Before - Leaving - Earth

This relates to being a man of God, a husband and being a father, but again they are only basic instructions.

(Verse from the Black and Brown Movement song "Giving Praise")

"We won't stop and we don't stop and we can't stop giving praise, B & B Movement session, God and his son's blessing, Jesus la luz with aggression,

He's needed, my heart bleeded when she greeted me with that ill negativity,

He got that remedy,

It'll never be able or capable to interrupt, corrupt or disrupt this man's vibe,

Descendent of the 7 tribes of Aztlan, from Africa to Mazatlán,

Pyramids rise like the sun from east to west, day to night,

Loyalty for his royalty, Lord you spoil me,

The devil tried to **FOIL** *me with his method **F** irst / **O** uter / **I** nner / **L** ast ,*

He got my head spinning, from the past to the future while he got me doing math,

I'd rather give praise, on my knees every night I pray.

I have had to look to God for strength, guidance, and wisdom, when there was no one else to look to in this world. I realized it was him I was to look to first anyway. I had to look to historical figures for examples of leadership, fortitude, integrity, and sacrifice. Some of those men I have mentioned previously, however my best role model has always been my Lord and savior Jesus Christ. He gave his life, to save our souls. There have been times in my life when I have felt that I was stumbling and struggling and could not get out of my own way. I feel like we as human beings, since the beginning of time, have gone further and further away from God. I believe that we as humans have lived for the creation of convenience and have made all the problems that we have today. We seem to always complicate things. We make them harder than they must be. We have practically destroyed this earth that was given to us as a gift.

We have lost nature in all our "development." I will never forget the two years I was blessed to spend in the National Park of Yosemite. I never felt closer to God as I was in his country and on his land. I remember hiking 75 miles in one day (Not by choice). I was part of the staff that year and we hiked twenty-five miles to camp at the base of Half Dome. (Thousands of years ago a giant glacier cut out the Yosemite Valley and Half Dome used to be a full dome) The only reason I hiked 75 miles that day was because somebody got lost on the way and only after hiking fifty miles, they inform me by radio that they had made it. Obviously, I had to hike twenty-five miles back to the base of Half Dome. The next day I climbed that giant piece of Granite five times with a one-hundred-pound backpack each time. There were people in our crew who wanted to camp on the top of Half Dome but feared heights and needed help up the rock. We sandwiched them up (Some one on each side of them and the other carried the pack). There were so many things done in Yosemite that helped to shape this individual warrior/worker, this now husband/father/brother/uncle who became a leader.

The Birth of a Movement

After the life experiences that included the family drama created by a negative spirit originated from the roots and spread through to the branches of our family tree and after the unorthodox journey from the light to the dark, from the classroom to the streets, from our neighborhood/training/stomping grounds and obstacle course of survival to out of town/state from L.A. to the Lou (Los Angeles to Saint Louis) and every stop in between. From letter to word to line to verse to song to demo to album to catalog. Our music has gone from nursery rhymes to Hip-Hop masterpieces, from poetry readings to spoken word recitals to freestyle sessions. There were the showcases and the auditions, and the small venue shows and the bigger club performances that all developed us as individual artists as well as a group. Whether it was a track produced by someone else or by Marques (Dank Right) or whether it was the live band playing behind us, we always rocked it to the best of our abilities!

(Excerpt from my poem "The young and Good")

"The Young and Good die hard! I ask why God? Must life be so rough and tough, haven't we struggled enough? Even though we don't have much, we still have good and plenty. We have a nickel when some have only got a penny. We have a quarter when some have only got a dime. It's all about havin thangs, you got yours and I've got mine. When will we ever be able to find that middle ground and be able to stand down as Black and Brown?"

CHAPTER 24

Nikki and I have been married for years now, we have four beautiful children and although it hasn't always been easy, we figured out how to get through the tough times and come out stronger on the other side. We have always been there for each other, whatever it was and through our flaws. We strengthen and balance each other. We love each other. We talk things out, work through things and we do our best not to stay mad at each other for long or go to bed mad. Parenting has been a challenge. Although Nik is "Super Mom," I had to learn the hard way, that just being present isn't enough. I had to be involved in my children's lives, in their heads, and in their feelings. I needed to be involved in their schooling. I had to make sure I taught my kids the lessons, morals, and virtues that I have learned along my way. Being a father has been one of the greatest blessings and pleasures in my life. I thank my parents for all they have done for me, to make me the man that I am today. Even though it wasn't always pretty, I know they did the best they could. I am an optimist, and the glass will always be half full, because something is always better than nothing, and growing up with nothing helps you to appreciate everything. My parents if nothing else showed me by example what to do in certain situations and what not to do when I became a parent. I believe that each generation should be better than the one before it. I pray that my children will be ten times better than me and I am already seeing it.

My mother still lives in the Bay Area with my sister Amber and my nephew Raphael and my niece Michigan. Amanda has gone on to graduate college and has gotten married. My mother has had some health issues but is doing good as she has stopped drinking and smoking cigarettes, years back now. She has had to change her lifestyle to maintain her health. We have gotten a bit closer over the years as she has opened and shared vital info to my self-discovery as well as vital insight into who she is as a person and not who she is as my mother. She is now retired.

I am extremely proud of my brother Silas who was married for about ten years and has been divorced for about that same length of time, with his two sons and the bitter custody and child support battles he has endured. He has also lived in the Bay Area for years now and without a college degree and only his high school diploma, has managed to build himself a career in the import/export industry as well as always having a side job. He has since gone back to school and has done his best to better himself. We have had our issues since Josiah's death, and we continue to work through them. He partially blamed me for Josiah's death as I did him as well and for the exact same reason. That incident when he convinced Josiah that they could make it on their own, when they were still staying with me. He felt that in that fallout, I chased them away as in the same instance I felt it was Silas that influenced Josiah to leave. We realized what we knew all along that those were not the reasons that Josiah was murdered. We know and believe in the fact that everything happens for a reason and that when it's your time, it's your time. The most we can hope for and have faith in is that we all meet up in the end.

My little sister Amber has gone through her journey that entailed being involved with a church that had their own business and entrenched her to a point where I believe she began to lose God as well as herself. There is one thing other than the lesson learned that I think she would agree, was a positive taken from that situation. That would be meeting the father of her first-born child and having my nephew, Rafael. I am just as proud of her, for all that she has accomplished to this point, such as an AA and BA degrees, a real estate license and becoming the woman she is today. We have had our issues like any other siblings and family members, and the one thing I have always told her is that she is my sister and I love her no matter what.

I am not as close with the rest of my family, that I would like to be, and must take my part in that. I am still working on my communication and being connected and seeing them more and putting in my efforts. Everyone has grown and has gotten better and that is a blessing to see.

Marques and I continue to work every angle we can regarding the music and the clothing line and the podcast and the Movement. And we continue to be the best men and fathers we can be. Marques has been through so much in his life, from the time we met until now. He has been battling major health issues over the years, physically and mentally. He was fighting to be in his daughter's lives and dealing with estranged relationships. He was shot again, one Thanksgiving Day we came back to the hood to meet up with the Jones family and the Barrigas (Black and Brown). We were chillin' outside drinking and smoking and someone from our hood had killed a rival earlier that day, down on Crenshaw and Jefferson at the Burger King, but they didn't think to come warn us that they had done so. A young rival came walking through our block and began shooting. Marques caught a bullet in his foot and Carlos Barriga caught one in his back. A few inches over, it would have hit his spine. Marques is one of the strongest and most faithful people I have ever known. I tell him all the time; I don't know how he made it through all he has been through. He says, "through the grace of GOD!" I have also told him many times, that he has always been a source of strength for me.

Ricky found his victory in his years long battle with drugs and has been clean and sober for years now. He has two jobs, one with the county of Los Angeles, working with the homeless population. He started with one job at a transitional housing facility and has worked his way up and is now a supervisor. He built his credit up and has a car and his own place. He continues to improve and work on his mental health, and we continue to work on our Movement. He had to deal with the deaths of his parents a short time apart. He left Washington state shortly after his mother's death and came back to LA, where he has built a life for himself, with a bright future.

Pops had been up in the Bay Area (San Francisco) for years, off drugs other than Methadone which is supposed to wean you off heroin. He got himself together somewhat, has an income, had a vehicle and was renting a room, until he started having issues at his dwelling. He ended up moving back down to LA and is currently staying with Ricky. We don't really talk or interact, and under the advice of my therapist, I do need closure with that relationship.

There are others that I have mentioned that are still around, like KiKi and Bruce. Money K and Avery are still in the picture, even though Avery and Money K both live in Arizona. The circle has gotten smaller and even though there have been a few that have come and gone in recent years, there is one that never strayed, Jerald Amaya aka "Darkside 90042," the self-proclaimed King of Northeast LA. This region of LA includes towns such as Highland Park and Echo Park.

Darkside is someone we met years ago at Cal State LA. I remember he was performing on the campus, and we approached him after the show. He was a father, an MC, a teacher, a member of the Hip Hop Caucus, a member of a couple of groups, one of the founders of A.U.E.H. (Artists United to END Homelessness) (which we the Movement are a part of now) and just an all-round good guy. He always involved us in whatever it was he was doing. He supported us and we supported him. He introduced us to numerous people in the underground Hip Hop scene of LA. Some of those people are L Scatter Brain, his group "Numerous," Lee Ballinger, one of the founders of A.U.E.H. He invited us to several events, where we met and networked with even more heads. He even let Marques stay with him in Highland Park when Marques was in transition at the time. I remember the last time I saw him. Lee Ballinger and someone else from A.U.E.H. went to his house since we were supposed to have a meeting. There was no parking around his apartment building, and he came outside and was coughing. He was sick at the time and wasn't looking so good. We told him to go back inside and suggested he go see a doctor. I want to say a week later, we found out he was diagnosed with Stage 4 stomach cancer. And only a couple of weeks after that, we were told that Jerald Amaya died at the age of forty, on Father's Day. We attended his funeral and a couple of tribute shows in his honor and will always be grateful that we met and knew him and will continue to miss him. We do what we do to honor him and his legacy, Josiah's legacy, Joey's legacy, Jah's legacy, and all those who impacted our lives and are no longer with us.

It was Silas who reminded me that what we have with this "Movement," is a brand, a lifestyle. As it is much more than the music, it's the social non-profit impact that we have had and have and can make. It's the multi-media and fashion facets of this endeavor that makes it a brand. It's the experience that is us and is always on display. I understand what he means for those on the outside looking in but really it was just us living, with what we were given. We were/are living the best way we knew/know how. It was and is what we have learned from so many different people that have come across our paths. Our makeup and how we are built comes from our unstable foundation and environment. We are imperfect and irregular and are proud of it. I wouldn't change a thing.

As I grew and got older, I had to learn how to get out of my own way. I used to think too much and used to over analyze. I would complicate things for myself and when I realized that it would take stripping things down to the bare bones and building the foundation from there, things became easier. I was no longer spreading myself thin and wearing myself out and taking the world on my shoulders. I realized that God would only give me what I can handle, and I know that did not mean every burden was mine to bear. No matter how big my heart is, it still only has a certain capacity.

I am not nor have I ever been or will I ever be perfect (along with the rest of humanity). In all my writing and rhyming and poetry, the blessing of it all was found in the "Good News," the "Gospel." This is where it is said that "Life and Death are in the Power of the Tongue." I always knew that applied to the words you would read in this story, and I discovered that my purpose, my work from this point will be solely focused on leaving my mark and leaving my legacy.

*E*PILOGUE

What will your legacy be?

Josiah's grandfather, Manasseh, was a violent King who filled "Jerusalem from one end to the other with the people's blood" (2 ki 21:16 NLT) His father, King Amon, died at the hands of his own officers. "He did what God said was wrong" reads his epitaph. Josiah was only eight when he ascended to the throne. Immediately he chose righteousness and did not stop doing what was right all his life (and 2 ki 22:2) What's the point? We cannot pick our parents, but we can pick our role models. When Josiah was rebuilding the temple, he discovered a scroll containing God's law. As he read it, he wept, realizing his people had drifted far from God. So, he sent word to a prophetess and asked, "what will become of our people?" She told Josiah that since he had repented when he heard God's word, his nation would be spared (see 2 ch 34:14-27) Wow! An entire generation received grace because of the integrity of one man. So, you can rise above your past and make a difference. Your parents may have given you your DNA, but God can give you a new birth and new beginning. "You are God's children whom he loves, so try to be like him" (Eph 5:1 NIV) Just like Josiah you cannot control the way your forefathers responded to God, but you can control the way you respond to him. Your past does not have to be your prison; you have a say in your life, you have a voice in your destiny, you have a choice in the path you take. Choose well and someday-generations from now-others will thank God for the legacy you left. (Literature from B.E.F.I.C. Bible Enrichment Fellowship International Church)

The legacy I leave is The Black and Brown Movement and only God knows where it goes when I am gone. However, the journey has been a blessing and I thank God for the birth of the Movement.

About the Author

De Franco Felipe Brocks Montemayor is a man of mixed racial and cultural make up and background. He was born in Los Angeles, California, where he has spent most of his life. He has diverse educational, cultural, and street experience. He has been creatively writing since he was twelve years old yet this is his first publication. He attended Humboldt State University, Cal State Northridge, East Los Angeles College, Los Angele Trade Technical College, and is now in the process of completing his bachelor's degree at Central State University (an HBCU Historical Black College University). He also rounded out his education at USC University of South Central, college of the streets. He is a son, a brother (oldest of five siblings), a cousin, an uncle, and a father. Most of all, he is a man who learned that to be a man was an honor, and along with that honor, comes responsibility. If it is not seen as an honor to be a man, the responsibility is not seen to be lived up to.